Stride:
The Music of
Fats Waller

Twayne's Music Series

Stride:
The Music of
Fats Waller

Paul S. Machlin

Twayne Publishers

Stride: The Music of Fats Waller

Paul S. Machlin

Copyright © 1985 by G. K. Hall & Company
All Rights Reserved
Published by Twayne Publishers
A Division of G. K. Hall & Company
70 Lincoln Street
Boston Massachusetts 02111

Printed on permanent/durable acid-free
paper and bound in the United States of
America.

Book production by Marne B. Sultz
Book design by Barbara Anderson

Library of Congress Cataloging in Publication Data

Machlin, Paul S.
Stride, the music of Fats Waller.

Bibliography: p. 114
Discography: p. 118
Includes index.
1. Waller, Fats, 1904–1943—Criticism and interpretation. 2. Jazz music—
Analysis, appreciation.
I. Title
ML417.W15M3   1985   785.42′092′4 [B]   85-7632
ISBN 0-8057-9468-9
ISBN 0–8057–9470–0 (pbk)

Contents

About the Author

Paul S. Machlin is currently associate professor of music and chairman of the department at Colby College in Waterville, Maine. He earned the Bachelor of Arts degree with honors in music from Yale University (1968) and the M.A. and Ph.D. degrees in music from the University of California at Berkeley (1969 and 1975, respectively). His dissertation is a study of the sketches and publication history of Richard Wagner's opera *The Flying Dutchman*, and he has published several articles and reviews on this and other Wagner topics.

In 1976 he designed and taught Colby's first course in jazz, and became especially intrigued with the language of stride piano. A preliminary investigation in 1979 of Waller's early solo recordings generated some of the seminal ideas on which the present study is based. Commenting on his shift from Wagner to Waller, a librarian friend of Prof. Machlin remarked, "I couldn't help noticing that you haven't moved out of the WA's yet." It was surely the kind of observation Waller himself would have approved of.

In addition to his teaching and administrative duties at Colby, Prof. Machlin is also director of the Colby College Chorale and the Waterville Area Community Chorus. He lives in Waterville with his wife, Susan Sterling, and his children, Gregory and Erica.

Preface

Stride piano music in general and Fats Waller's work in particular form a discrete and important current running through the mainstream of jazz, not just an insignificant tributary. But although Waller's popularity was enormous during his brief lifetime, and his influence considerable, there exist only two biographies, which, while helpful in establishing a chronological outline of the events of Waller's life, avoid any detailed discussion of his music. (The authors of these two biographies are Waller's son, Maurice, and his manager, Ed Kirkeby [see Bibliography]. A third book, *Fats Waller: His Life and Times,* by Joel Vance, is apparently based on Kirkeby's account, but Vance unfortunately seeks rather too aggressively to advance his hypothesis that the death of Waller's mother constituted a severe psychological trauma in his youth from which he never recovered. Consequently, Vance interprets the style and substance of Waller's adulthood—particularly his humor and showmanship—as a mask for his supposed emotional immaturity. It is an untenable proposition at best.) In fact, apart from Morroe Berger's brief but telling analysis of Waller's verbal asides and interpolations, no attempt to examine his music in depth has, to my knowledge, been published. Part of the reason for this dearth of critical study lies, I suspect, in the persistent myths surrounding Waller's life—myths that magnify his affinity and capacity for high living, his conviviality, his ebullient personality, and his supposed disinclination to take his music seriously. Thus inflated, these attributes have overshadowed both the quality of his improvisations and the magnitude of his contributions to jazz.

This book is a study of Fats Waller's music, with an emphasis on those works from his monumental output that have hitherto not received critical attention—the pre-1930 piano solos, the solo pipe organ music, and certain seminal interpretations from the last decade of his life. The piano solos of his first maturity demonstrate the wealth of Waller's invention as a composer and improviser and his exceptional skill as a performer. His pipe organ recordings provide evidence of his ability to adapt the principles and techniques of stride piano to a different (albeit related) medium. And a significant portion of his later work, especially the infrequently recorded alternate takes of this period, which document Waller's varying interpretations of a piece, reveals a developing harmonic freedom, a newfound predilection for extended melodic lines, and the emergence of an introspective and understated style. In the final analysis, then, a meaningful account of Waller's achievement as a jazz composer and improviser must come to terms with the music preserved in these performances; careful listening to them is repaid with multiple aural riches. For with Waller, it's really a very simple matter: what you hear is what you get. One need only pay close heed to his own advice, offered at the opening of his very first solo vocal recording, "I'm Crazy 'Bout My Baby": "Listen, can you stand me to tell you about it? Listen here. . . ."

Paul S. Machlin

Colby College

Acknowledgments

Perhaps the most gratifying aspect of jazz research is the number of friendly and helpful people one encounters. I have received guidance and assistance in this project from a broad spectrum of professionals and aficionados whose warmth and infectious enthusiasm made my tasks pleasant ones.

I must thank first my parents, Stuart and Evangeline Machlin—especially my father, who introduced me to Fats Waller on record. (He also introduced my mother to Waller's music, but that was at a show at the Apollo Theater in Harlem in the 1930s, and she thus had the good fortune to hear Waller in person.)

Anyone who does research in jazz must inevitably come to rely on the vast and splendid resources of the Institute of Jazz Studies on the Newark campus of Rutgers University, and on its knowledgeable staff. Ed Berger answered with dispatch and clarity countless inquiries ranging from the minutiae of discographical and bibliographical citations to broader questions concerning style and influence. The institute's director, Dan Morgenstern, generously gave me access to papers and memorabilia in the institute's collection from the estate of Ed Kirkeby, Waller's last manager. Other archivists and librarians have rendered assistance with the goodwill that seems to characterize members of that profession: Susan Sommer, Head of Special Collections, Music Division, New York Public Library; Connell Gallagher, Curator of Manuscripts at the Bailey/Howe Library, University of Vermont; Keith Stetson, Leah Emdy, and Ann Basart, all of the Music Library, University of California, Berkeley; and Marilyn R. Pukkila of Miller Library at Colby. My friends and colleagues Stephen Nuthall, Bruce Stewart, Tim Hunt, and Lewis Porter, and my father-in-law, Jack Sterling, have helped locate recordings of obscure and difficult to acquire Waller performances. I also turned on occasion to two scholars of twentieth-century American music, Professors Lawrence Starr and James McCalla, whose suggestions proved invaluable.

During the summer of 1983, Glen Wright, a music major at Colby College, served as my research assistant for the compilation of the Waller discography included in this volume. Undaunted by the mass of information involved (and by the long hours required to put it into a coherent format), Glen worked tirelessly and diligently throughout the summer and on into the fall of his senior year to complete the project. Without his computer expertise and assistance, I cannot imagine a finished product half so cogently organized. (Of course, any errors in the final version are fully my own responsibility.) Glen's position was funded by a grant from Colby; for this and other grants from the College (notably from Colby's Humanities Grants Committee, to cover travel expenses incurred through trips to New York and Newark), I am grateful, especially to Professor Douglas Archibald, Dean of Faculty at Colby. (During many of those trips, I took advantage of hospitality offered by my friends Stephanie and Roger Traub, Mark Pecker and Betsey McGee, and Jay and Suzie Sterling.) In addition, Professors James Armstrong and Peter Ré, then colleagues in Colby's music department, gave me welcome encouragement and advice; Mrs. Helen Staples, the music department secretary, saw to it with her usual consummate skill that the department continued to operate smoothly during my first year as chairman, which was also my last year of working on the book. (Indeed, in many ways, Helen *is* the music department.)

A National Endowment for the Humanities Fellowship for College Teachers, awarded for the 1982–83 academic year, enabled me to write the major portion of this book during my sabbatical leave. Also while on sabbatical, I interviewed James Roseveare, organist at the Paramount Theater in Oakland, California, who helped identify some of Waller's registrations and clarified for me both verbally and by demonstration the characteristics of the theater organ style.

My editor at Twayne, John LaBine, has been an understanding and sympathetic advocate, effectively representing my concerns to G. K. Hall, graciously assenting to the more intractable of my demands, and patiently coaxing me to meet my deadlines. My typist at Colby, Karen Bourassa, performed with what to me was miraculous Waller-like speed and dexterity on the keyboard (of her word-processor). Frances Waner's counsel and guidance were, as always, penetrating, practical, and wise.

My wife, Susan Sterling, to whom this book is dedicated, edited the entire manuscript with profound understanding, respect for my intentions, apparently boundless energy, and a scrupulously impartial eye. As a critic of writing she is peerless—friendly but firm in offering suggestions for improvement; always right in matters of sense and substance, yet never dogmatic or inflexible about style; ever optimistic that solutions to syntactical problems can be found, but never content to leave such problems until they have, in fact, been solved. She has the enviable ability to take often muddled and half-formed thoughts and give them a prose shape that suits and expresses them perfectly. But of course, Sue did much more than editing. Sharing my enthusiasm for the music, she took an active interest in all stages of the work, including the formative ones; our conversations about Waller have brought my own ideas more sharply into focus. At the same time, she helped me keep this project in perspective so that I was able to balance my time at work with time for my family. For all this I owe her thanks; it is a debt of gratitude that I bear with great happiness.

Portions of this manuscript appeared in different form in papers read at the 1979 and 1983 annual meetings of the American Musicological Society.

"Spreadin' Rhythm Around" copyright 1935 (©Renewed 1963) Robbins Music Corporation. Rights of Robbins Music Corporation assigned to CBS Catalogue Partnership. All rights controlled and administered by CBS Robbins Catalog Inc. International Copyright Secured. All Rights Reserved. Used By Permission. "I'm Crazy 'Bout My Baby (And My Baby's Crazy 'Bout Me)," words by Alexander Hill, music by Thomas Waller. Copyright 1931 Edwin H. Morris & Company, a division of MPL Communications, Inc. © Renewed 1959 Edwin H. Morris & Company, a division of MPL Communications, Inc. International Copyright Secured. All Rights Reserved. Used By Permission. "Inside (This Heart of Mine)," words by J. C. Johnson, music by Thomas Waller; used by Permission of the Publisher. Belwin Mills Publishing Corporation, Melville, N.Y.

Chronology

1904   Thomas Wright Waller born in New York City to Edward and Adeline Waller, 21 May (probably at 107 West 134th Street in Harlem).

ca. 1909–1910   Waller's father introduces him to the harmonium; he accompanies the family's singing at streetcorner sermons.

1910–1911   After Waller shows interest in a neighbor's piano, his family acquires one. He starts lessons with a Miss Perry, a local teacher.

ca. 1918   At Public School 89, the music teacher, Miss Corlias, encourages Waller to study violin and string bass.

1918   His father takes him to see the pianist Ignace Paderewski at Carnegie Hall.

1919   Plays in his first band at a streetcorner party. Meets Edith Hatch (whom he is later to marry). After becoming friendly with Mazie Mullins, the organist at Harlem's Lincoln Theater, Waller is occasionally allowed to play the music at intermission. Later, he assumes responsibility for the organ accompaniment to the theater's live vaudeville show.

1920   Mother dies of a stroke brought on by diabetes, 10 November. Leaves home and moves in with the family of a friend, Russell Brooks. Discovers some piano rolls cut by James P. Johnson. By alternately starting and stopping the piano mechanism, teaches himself Johnson's technique, placing his fingers on those keys that have been activated by the mechanism. Later, probably within the year, begins to study stride piano seriously with Johnson. Marries Edith Hatch.

1921   First son, Thomas Waller, Jr., is born. Goes on tour with the vaudeville troupe "Liza and Her Shufflin' Six."

On this same tour, meets Bill (Count) Basie in Boston; later gives Basie organ lessons at the Lincoln Theater. Plays his first "rent party."

1923   Edith Hatch Waller seeks and obtains a divorce from her husband. Waller wins a piano competition at the Roosevelt Theater in New York with his version of Johnson's "Carolina Shout." (Other sources, notably John Chilton, in *Who's Who of Jazz,* have suggested an earlier date— 1918—for the contest.) Meets Andrea Menentania (or Andreamentena) Razafinkeriefo (or Razafinkieriefo) (Andy Razaf), a lyricist with whom he is to write many songs. Meets Louis Armstrong.

1924   Begins frequenting Connie's Inn, a Harlem nightclub, where he meets George Maines, who acts as an adviser to Waller in both his personal and professional affairs. Waller, as "Ali-baba, the Egyptian Wonder," plays the Kentucky Club, another Harlem nightclub, with Duke Ellington's band.

1925   Travels with Louis Armstrong to Chicago. (He is reputed during his time in Chicago to have studied piano with Leopold Godowsky.)

1926   Marries Anita Rutherford. With Spencer Williams, writes the scores for "Tan Topics" and "Junior Blackbirds," two all-black revues. Briefly joins Fletcher Henderson's band.

1927   Maurice Thomas Waller is born to Anita and Thomas Waller. Waller plays the Vendome Theater in Chicago with the Erskine Tate Orchestra, February.

1928   Ronald Waller, second son to Anita and Thomas, is born. Waller, with Andy Razaf, writes half the score to "Keep Shufflin'." The other half is composed by James P. Johnson, with lyrics by Henry Creamer and Clarence Todd. Substitutes for James P. Johnson in a concert of blues, spirituals, and jazz at Carnegie Hall, New York, 27 April. Gets a job playing organ and piano at the Royal Grand Theater in Philadelphia. Sentenced to a jail term for failure to make alimony payments to Edith Waller, his first wife. (Chilton suggests 1927 for this event.) Probably incarcerated for some period between Octo-

ber 1928 and 1 March 1929, when he participated in a
recording session for Victor. His father dies. Writes
part of the revue "Load of Coal" with Andy Razaf.

1929 Writes score to "Hot Chocolates" with Andy Razaf. In
order to avoid legal difficulties stemming from charges
of nonsupport brought by Edith, hastily raises the sum
of five hundred dollars by selling rights to twenty of his
popular songs. This amount represents a fraction of
their potential value.

1930 Secures his own radio show, "Paramount on Parade,"
with the help of manager Joe Davis; show runs from December 1930 through June 1931.

1931 Meets pianist Art Tatum. Plays on radio show "Radio
Roundup," and works at the Hotfeet Club in Greenwich
Village. Sings for the first time on a recording (with the
Ted Lewis Band): "I'm Crazy 'Bout My Baby."

1932 Travels to Paris with Spencer Williams (August–September). Phil Ponce becomes his manager. Moves to
Cincinnati, Ohio, to work for radio station WLW. Is giv-
en his own program, "Fats Waller's Rhythm Club." Also
plays organ on a program of his own called "Moon River," aired late at night, but receives no credit from the
station as the performer on this program.

1934 Receives extensive publicity through a series of radio
appearances in New York (March–April).

1935 Travels to Hollywood to be filmed for brief appearances
in two films, *King of Burlesque* and *Hooray for Love*
(probably June).

1938 Makes a second European trip, visiting London and appearing with the Mills Brothers. Here he composes the
"London Suite," a series of short piano vignettes in a
jazz idiom. He also tours the Continent and Scandinavia
(July–October). Ed Kirkeby becomes his manager. (It
is likely that Kirkeby began informally assuming some
managerial duties as early as 1935.)

1939 Makes his last European sojourn, touring England, the
Continent, and Scandinavia. In one instance, he is re-
puted narrowly to have avoided a confrontation with
Nazi troops.

1942   Presents a concert in Carnegie Hall, 14 January. Although apparently well received by the audience, at least one critic (Mark Schubart) gave a mixed review of the concert. (*PM Daily* 2, no. 15 [Thursday, 15 January 1942]:24).

1943   Writes music for the show "Early to Bed," which opens in Boston. Travels to Hollywood in January, arriving 20 January, where he is filmed with Lena Horne, Bill "Bojangles" Robinson, and others for an appearance in *Stormy Weather*. Returns to Hollywood in the fall for an engagement at the Zanzibar Room; falls ill during the engagement. Aboard the passenger train Santa Fe Chief, en route from Los Angeles to New York, dies (probably of pneumonia) on the night of 14–15 December; his death is discovered the morning of 15 December in Kansas City, Missouri.

1

"Exuberance is the Spontaneity of Life"

Music everywhere, feet are pattin',
Puttin' tempo in old Manhattan,
Everybody is out high hattin',
Spreadin' rhythm around.

Everywhere you go trumpets blarin',
Drums and saxophones rippin' and tearin',
Everybody you meet is rarin',
Spreadin' rhythm around.

Up in Harlem, in any flat, they give you that thing
Which according to one and all is what they call swing—

Those who can't afford silks and satin,
Dames with gigolos who are Latin,
Come from Yonkers, the Bronx and Staten—
Spreadin' rhythm around.

"Spreadin' Rhythm Around,"
music by Jimmy McHugh, lyrics by Ted Koehler

Harlem: the spiritual, cultural, and intellectual center of urban life for pre-
and post-Depression black Americans; the fabled nucleus of sensational and
forbidden pleasures for white society's urban upper crust who came there to
savor, among other experiences, sensual and exotic nightclub extravagan-
zas. This New York City district, centered around the intersection of 125th
Street and Lenox Avenue in northern Manhattan, was both home to Thomas
Wright "Fats" Waller for most of his life and the focal point of his creative

activity. Small wonder it should nourish him—numerous contemporary accounts, both fictional and documentary, as well as recently published chronicles, describe a rapidly growing, energetic community where blacks, freed from the necessity to seek an identity or a position in society, could, if they so chose, simply get on with their lives in whatever manner pleased them. In Harlem, they stood at least a fair chance of fashioning their own destiny; although there may have been an equal likelihood of failure as of success, of leading a life of severe deprivation and destitution, many blacks apparently perceived Harlem as an environment that erected fewer obstacles to their individual and social progress than others. And Harlem was also home to blacks who either had attained some measure of recognition through economic success or had had a distinctive cultural status bestowed on them by their own well-received literary or artistic endeavors. Such success and status could be taken as an incentive to young black citizens, especially those from a middle-class background, to attempt to follow similar paths. Thus, all strata of black society, from the very wealthy to the indigent, from the cultivated to those whose pursuits were more earthy, chose to inhabit Harlem, transforming this hitherto unprepossessing section of New York City into a microcosm of black urban life in the early twentieth century.

Just as the United States attracted immigrants from abroad in the nineteenth and twentieth centuries, so Harlem attracted blacks from all parts of the United States. Among these migrants, Edward and Adeline Waller came to New York from Virginia in 1888 in order to raise their children in a place where at least a modicum of educational opportunity was available to them. They were both sixteen years old at the time, and they settled first in Greenwich Village, a black neighborhood in those years.[1] The Wallers moved uptown to West Sixty-third Street, probably in 1892 or 1893. By this time three sons, one of whom died in infancy, had been born to the couple. (Eventually, Adeline gave birth to eleven children, only five of whom survived.) The family appears to have relocated to Harlem around 1902, to 28 West 134th Street. At some point before Thomas Waller's birth, they moved again to a different apartment in the same neighborhood, at 107 West 134th Street. (They may also have lived in other apartments before settling at the final 134th Street location.)[2] Waller's parents chose Greenwich Village originally because the Abyssinian Baptist Church, with which they affiliated themselves, was located there. The couple made the subsequent moves in order to be near the church, which itself moved uptown twice—first to Eighth Avenue and West 40th Street, and then to Harlem.

Like many blacks in a similar economic and social situation, both Edward and Adeline were musical as well as devout, and the value they accorded music in a religious context informed their daily lives. Evidently, this regard for music had its most profound impact on their son Thomas, of all their children; possibly as early as his fifth or sixth year, he is reported to have played the harmonium (see chapter 3, note 2) to accompany his family's singing at streetcorner sermons delivered by his father. (By this time, the family had transferred their membership to a different church, and Edward had become a lay preacher.)[3] Thus the environments that helped shape Thomas's life in these years included his home, the church, the street, and, to a lesser extent, his school. He started piano lessons with Miss Perry, a local teacher, in 1910 or 1911, but dropped them after a short while. Even at this early stage, he apparently showed a marked preference for popular music. He may also have occasionally been permitted to play the organ in his family's church; certainly, his most regular exposure to nonvernacular music occurred there.[4]

Waller's education in music began to intensify when he reached his mid-teens in 1919 and 1920. He studied and played both pipe organ and stride piano in earnest for the first time. His work on the organ led directly to his engagement at Harlem's Lincoln Theater; the live audience he played for undoubtedly brought out the comic and the theatrical in his nature. On the other hand, his study of stride piano seems to have been methodical and private—up to a point. He learned the basic techniques of stride playing from James P. Johnson, at that time the undisputed master of the style, and its probable progenitor as well. Possibly, Waller also learned some technical skills from piano rolls: he could memorize chord structures and figuration by advancing the roll very slowly, stopping for each new chord and placing his fingers over the keys activated by the roll mechanism. Eventually, he became accomplished and confident enough to play at rent parties (see Chapter 2), and the demands of those engagements helped to hone his already considerable performing strengths.

Waller became increasingly recognized in the early 1920s as a talented pianist, and as a result, increasingly busy. He cut his first record late in 1922, sometime in October (or possibly in December). In 1923, he made a number of piano rolls, and over the next few years, he accompanied several different blues singers at recording sessions. During this time, he continued to play for rent parties, but broadened his audience by performing at nightclubs, gaining some welcome professional exposure. In 1926 he composed the music for two revues with Spencer Williams; he had already composed dozens of songs by this time, both published and unpublished, but he apparently never copyrighted any material from this period, preferring rather to sell his compositions outright to a publisher for immediate cash, or perform them himself without troubling to see to their eventual publication. In any event, he mastered the crucial art of Tin Pan Alley songwriting, and through the quantity and quality of material he turned out, he began to acquire a reputation as the composer of reliably catchy and well-crafted songs; commissions to compose other revues followed in 1928 and 1929.

In fact, 1929 was in many ways a watershed year for Waller. First, it was the last year before 1934 in which he was involved in regular and extensive recording sessions throughout the year (in March, August, September, and December). Second, most of the performances recorded at these sessions were piano solos. This would be one of the few really comprehensive series of solo recordings Waller would make in his career, and it occurred during a period when his gifts as a composer and improviser meshed with his highly developed skills as a stride pianist, equipping him to achieve a consistently high level of originality as well as technical proficiency in his performances. Third, 1929 was one of Waller's most productive years as a composer; some of his finest songs, both published and unpublished, were composed in this year. (The list includes "Ain't Misbehavin'," "I've Got a Feeling I'm Falling," "Honeysuckle Rose," "(What Did I Do to Be So) Black and Blue?," "The Minor Drag," "Valentine Stomp," "Numb Fumblin'," and "Gladyse.") Finally, Waller made some ensemble recordings (on 30 September 1929) with a group that included Jack Teagarden, Eddie Condon, and Gene Krupa. Although this was not the first time Waller had recorded with white musicians, and although it may not have been the earliest association between top-ranked jazz musicians of the black and white races, it was one of the first occasions on which the black musician was given top billing in the group's title: "Fats Waller and His Buddies."

It is possible that the great reduction in Waller's recording activity is in some way attributable to the stock market crash of 1929, but it may also be a case of coincidental phenomena: Waller had other opportunities to pursue in 1930. He went on tour with the company of "Hot Chocolates," a revue for which he had composed the score in 1929. He also played at the Regal Theater in Chicago. At the close of the year, Waller undertook a commitment to appear on radio—a move that would enable him to exploit more fully than he previously had his talents as an entertainer. Between December 1930 and June 1931 Waller was featured on a short radio program, "Paramount on Parade," broadcast on the Columbia-owned station WABC.[5] In radio broadcasting, unlike live performance or recording situations, it was necessary to retain almost constant verbal contact with the audience, sometimes at the expense of the music itself. Waller's effusive wit thus found an ideal outlet in going on the air. He polished his style as a singer, making his first recording as a vocalist in 1931. From 1932 to 1934 he continued his radio broadcasting, first in Cincinnati, and later, in 1934, in New York.

All this exposure doubtless increased his fame and popularity, and must have influenced executives at the Victor Talking Machine Company in their decision to offer Waller a contract, which gave them the exclusive right to record him. Of course, the company also gained the power to control the repertoire and the musical arrangements Waller recorded; because the company's choices were based on commercial considerations, the bulk of Waller's Victor material consists of Tin Pan Alley songs (literally hundreds of them), arranged in one of a few standard formats, performed by Waller and usually five other musicians under the name "Fats Waller and His Rhythm." Although a number of different jazz musicians of varying degrees of talent performed as members of this group, Waller's most frequent partners in the Victor sessions were Herman Autrey (trumpet), Gene Sedric (clarinet, tenor sax), Albert Casey (guitar—occasionally, in 1939 and 1940, substituted for by John Smith), Charles Turner (bass), replaced by Cedric Wallace in 1939, and Slick Jones (drums). Together they formed a tight, well-rehearsed group that played competently and could be relied on to dispose of its musical obligations efficiently—in one take—but never lost its ability to improvise. But what we hear of the group on the issued and unissued takes, although often interesting and occasionally impressive, probably represents something less than its best efforts. I suspect that most of these musicians welcomed the recording sessions at Victor as an economic boon, but regarded them in musical terms as too restrictive. Doubtless on their own, in situations where they had control over their material and over the length of their solos, they achieved more compelling performances than those preserved on the Victor sides.

The association with Victor ushered in a new, comparatively long, and destructively hectic phase of Waller's career. The number and kinds of engagements he was offered increased: he went to Hollywood in 1935 and again in 1943 for appearances in films; he toured various parts of the United States; he toured Europe twice, in 1938 and 1939; and he continued to appear frequently on radio and in nightclubs. In addition, he fulfilled a series of recording obligations to Victor, which, in conjunction with all his other activity, turned his schedule into one of virtually perpetual performance. From 1935 to 1942, Waller went to the recording studio six times each year, on average—roughly every other month—making from six to ten or more takes each session. (And that rough statistical profile does not include [1] the series of recordings Waller made during each of his London visits, [2] the sessions for Associated Transcriptions, or [3] the V-discs cut toward the end of his career.) It is hardly surprising that such feverish activity adversely affected Waller's health, already severely taxed by probable overindulgence in food and liquor.

Yet Waller still found time to compose individual songs as well as the score for the show "Early to Bed." He even experimented with writing a piano suite in a jazz idiom; on his second European tour, in London in June 1939, Waller sketched and recorded six short piano solos he called collectively "The London Suite."[6] The title for each piece was taken from the name of a London district, a scheme probably suggested by Ed Kirkeby, Waller's manager at the time. (Although Waller did not invest the "Suite" with any genuinely significant compositional innovations, he did employ a different phrase and chorus structure for all but two of the pieces, "Soho" and "Limehouse." We can thereby deduce that he gave at least more than passing thought to the composition of the pieces.) And Waller occasionally played and sang something other than the usual (and, toward the end of his career, increasingly banal) repertoire of popular songs Victor had committed itself to. At a session on 20 November 1939, during which he made several sixteen-inch Lang-Worth transcription discs, Waller recorded spirituals, folk songs, and excerpts from well-known operas, using their themes as the basis for jazz interpretations. There was by this time, of course, a well-established and accepted tradition of jazzing the classics—i.e., playing excerpts from the standard repertory of works by nineteenth-century European composers in a jazz idiom. (Other kinds of cross-fertilization between the two musics occurred as well; often, the central thematic material from a well-known work in the classical repertoire, for example, might reappear as the melody of a popular song. In one memorable instance, however, Waller, in a clever and appealing reversal of this process, generates from the theme of one of his own popular songs, "Honeysuckle Rose," the material for a mock-sophisticated, classically styled rhapsody he titled "Honeysuckle Rose, à la Bach, Beethoven, Brahms, and Waller," recorded 13 May 1941, matrix no. 063890-1.)

At the beginning of 1943, Waller journeyed to California in order to appear in the film *Stormy Weather*, an all-black musical whose cast included Lena Horne, Bill "Bojangles" Robinson, Cab Calloway, the Nicholas Brothers, Dooley Wilson, and other star entertainers. Although his health was declining noticeably, he returned to Hollywood in October for an engagement at the Zanzibar Room, but became ill while there. He continued to work at the club after some rest, but he had probably not fully recovered: on the return trip to New York, during the night of 14–15 December 1943, he died on board the train, apparently of pneumonia. His funeral, appropriately enough, was held at the Abyssinian Baptist Church on 138th Street in Harlem, the church his parents had originally been affiliated with after moving uptown before Thomas's birth. Over 4,200 people were estimated to have attended the funeral; as the Reverend Dr. Adam Clayton Powell remarked in his eulogy, "Fats Waller always played to a packed house."[7]

2

Waller Strides Forward

Like the work of many great jazz musicians, Waller's output was conditioned in part by economic considerations: his buoyant style of performance animated the hundreds of trivial songs he recorded for Victor in the 1930s, and it was through them that he achieved commercial success, while his earlier work on piano and pipe organ remained in obscurity. But clever and captivating though Waller's performances are in the later recordings, they sometimes mask his most significant talents—those of a gifted and highly skilled stride pianist. Stride piano refers both to a technique and a style of jazz piano playing that flourished in New York City in the 1920s and 1930s. The technique, whose roots lie in the formal gestures of ragtime composition, centers on a basic left-hand pattern: the alternation of a fundamental pitch, placed deep in the bass range of the piano and played on the strong beats of a 4/4 measure (beats 1 and 3), with a chord that fills out and more completely identifies the same harmony, played in the tenor or mid-range of the piano on weak beats (beats 2 and 4). Thus, the left hand is continually shifting its position, "striding" back and forth over the left half of the keyboard.

But although the essence of this technique derives from ragtime, it is marked by a number of significantly different characteristics. A typical ragtime left-hand pattern, for example, uses a single pitch or an octave (a doubling of the single pitch) for the fundamental note (Example 2.1a); a stride pattern (Example 2.1b) will often enlarge the interval from an octave to a tenth and add a third pitch between the two outer ones, enriching the texture and identifying the harmony on the strong beat. Furthermore, a stride pianist will often roll such chords (i.e., play them one note at a time in rapid succession, from bottom to top), providing a greater sense of forward momentum and swing. In ragtime, the left-hand pattern is completed by chords

Example 2.1a

Example 2.1b

that appear on the offbeat and tend to be formed from the basic triad of the harmony involved. In stride, these chords often incorporate sevenths, ninths, blue notes, or other unexpected pitches only distantly related to the particular harmony in question; such chords, more complex than their ragtime counterparts, create a more subtly toned harmonic palette with a wider variety of sonorities.

These two examples of left-hand patterns, although they illustrate primarily some of the technical skills that distinguish stride from ragtime, can also serve to suggest the nature of larger stylistic differences between the two genres. Ragtime pieces are composed and are intended to be played exactly as notated by the composer. Stride playing, on the other hand, involves improvising—that is, spontaneously elaborating—on a preexisting piece. (The degree of spontaneity in the improvisation is certainly arguable, but that the performer substitutes music of his own creation for previously composed material is generally not.) Stride originated to a large extent in the social milieu of Harlem's informal nightlife—specifically, at rent parties (or rent socials, as they were sometimes called). Needy tenants would organize these gatherings in order to generate the capital necessary to pay a landlord another month's rent. The apartment where the party was to be held had to have a piano, since dancing was the primary form of entertainment, and the tenant would provide food and drink, and would hire the musician (or musicians). A small entrance fee was charged; by advertising the date of the party in advance (and perhaps the name of the pianist, if he was well known), the tenant could attract a crowd sizable enough to make a profit, which would cover the rent.

The pianist's major responsibility at these affairs was to insure that the music, proceeding continuously, facilitated constant dancing. Since rent parties often lasted through the night and well into the next morning, the pianist's musical imagination was taxed to its fullest. In order to keep the music fresh and vital, and to keep the dancers' energy from flagging, improvisation became a practical as well as an aesthetic necessity. Even so, few musicians would be capable of turning out a series of completely original improvisations for several hours without some form of preconceived material at their command. To meet this challenge, stride pianists developed repertoires of gestures or "tricks"—brief, decorative figures (just a few notes in some instances) usually but not exclusively for the right hand. These gestures were short enough to be repeated several times over the stride bass pattern as it passed through the harmonic changes of a phrase. Thus, the same figure could be used in almost any context, either alone or combined with any other gestures, to produce a long line of artful decoration requiring an impressive technique.

Improvisation in stride piano playing, then, consisted in part of the application of previously composed figures to a given melodic line so as to decorate and reshape it. In one sense, of course, this kind of elaboration on a preexisting melody was not "spontaneous," since the figures had already been prepared in the pianist's mind and fingers. Indeed, probably all jazz musicians construct just such a repertoire of ready-made gestures and use them to varying degrees in their improvisations. However, the particular gestures used, the subtle variations in shape and timing incorporated into them, and the way in which they are applied to the line all represent spontaneous choices by the musician; at least, such tends to be the procedure with stride pianists.

The technique of stride, then, helped a pianist in his job of providing an entire night of continuous music at a rent party. Frequently, too, the host would engage two or three stride pianists instead of just one to ensure that the music remained fresh and exciting. In such situations, the second pianist would relieve the first when he grew tired. (Sometimes, just to show off, the musicians performed this changing of the guard while a song was in progress, without a break in the music. This complicated maneuver would be accomplished one hand at a time. The pianist going off duty would slide over, continuing to play only with his right hand. At the instant he stopped playing with his left hand, the new pianist's left hand took over without skipping a beat; this procedure was then repeated for the right hand.) The third pianist would relieve the second in the same way, the first would eventually take over from the third, and the music thus became continuous. Clearly, competition was built into this kind of rotation. At rent parties, or in almost any other performance situation in which a number of pianists played consecutively, the competition was referred to as a "cutting contest." Each pianist would try to outdo ("cut") his predecessors in the complexity and sophistication of his tricks, and each developed, as a result, an individual, unmistakable style. The greater the difficulty of the music performed, the greater the stature accorded the pianist. Cutting contests thus had a significant effect on the development of stride, especially since a high degree of technical dexterity and an abundance of fresh ideas for improvisations were required to participate.[1]

Waller was introduced to rent parties and cutting contests during the early 1920s by his friend and mentor, James P. Johnson. Eventually, he became one of the three undisputed masters of Harlem stride piano, along with Johnson and Willie "the Lion" Smith. But during his apprenticeship as a stride pianist—a period that lasted, on the evidence of his recordings, until the mid-1920s—a variety of forces in addition to the cutting contests worked to sharpen his technique, increase his repertoire, and shape many elements of his style. His work as an organist, begun at the Lincoln Theater in Harlem in 1919,[2] and continued later at the Lafayette Theater, must have increased his skill at generating new ideas because it placed him in a situation (i.e., accompanying silent films) in which he had to improvise. In addition, it probably gave him a measure of security crucial to a young, relatively unknown performer playing his first major job before the public: the audience often included school friends who had come expressly to hear him play, and they are reported to have encouraged him by enthusiastically shouting "Hey, Fats, make it rock!"[3]

Waller's early, pre-1927 work in the recording studio may have had a less direct but still important effect on his playing. Recording sessions by and large were commercial, not artistic, ventures in which time was money. Musicians who recorded popular music had to produce an acceptable version of the piece they were recording on the first attempt, if possible, playing cleanly and crisply, with a minimum of rehearsal in the studio. Waller's facility was such that for these early recordings he rarely rehearsed at all before arriving at the studio for a session, yet he was still able to play almost flawlessly on the first take. There were other temporal considerations, too: Waller had to circumscribe his improvisations to fit them into the few measures (or, in the case of his two 1922 piano solos, into the time limit) allotted for his solo. Also, he had to discipline himself to match his style to the group or individual with whom he was recording.

On the majority of the early recordings (i.e., those made before 1927), Waller accompanied several different blues singers.[4] His work at these sessions demonstrates that he was already a sensitive if somewhat inexperienced accompanist: he could both double the melodic line with great subtlety, supporting but not overpowering the singer ("You've Got Ev'ry-thing a Sweet Daddy Needs but Me," with Sara Martin, 1 December 1922, matrix no. 71069-B) and provide a delicate counterpoint to the melody ("'Tain't Nobody's Business If I Do," matrix no. 71068-C, also with Sara Martin on the same date). He knew how to follow the singer faithfully in terms of tempo and phrasing, adjusting his pace to hers as necessary. If the singer's melody ended before the close of a phrase, he learned to fill in the break with stride gestures that complemented the melody. Finally, he learned the art of transposition, shifting the key of a song (and hence the entire accompaniment) up or down to match the singer's range. This last ability requires both a thorough grounding in music theory and technical skill, because playing the same piece in a new key means instituting a complete change in the usual fingerings.[5] (Waller may have undertaken some formal study of music theory at the Juilliard School of Music in 1925 with Carl Bohm;[6] such instruction would almost certainly have covered the theoretical principles governing transposition.)

Undoubtedly Waller's most important formal instruction during his apprenticeship came from James P. Johnson. Johnson is usually honored as the father of stride piano; born ten years before Waller, he was among the first of the Harlem pianists to develop a new jazz style for the instrument. This style was based, as we have seen, on the foundations of ragtime, requiring the same impressive technical dexterity as its predecessor, but with a looser, more swinging rhythmic drive. When Waller first began studying with Johnson, at about age seventeen, he lacked a knowledge of basic left-hand stride patterns. May Wright Johnson, James P.'s wife, suggested that Waller's extensive experience playing the pipe organ was responsible: "Of course you know the organ doesn't give you a left hand and that's what James P. had to teach him."[7] She was probably referring to the fact that Waller had learned to use the organ's pedals (manipulated with the feet) in place of training his left hand to perform some of the basic stride functions. From Johnson, Waller gained a relaxed, powerfully swinging left hand—accurate, even when it had to routinely span the interval of a tenth or more. Johnson also taught him to vary stride patterns, to suspend their use with breathtaking abruptness at crucial points of articulation when appropriate, and to syncopate them for increased rhythmic vigor.

Waller himself clearly appreciated the value of a solid left-hand technique. But the significance of the left hand in stride for Waller goes beyond mere fluency in reproducing stride patterns. His son Maurice has commented, "The thing I remember most emphatically from what my father used to show me is the importance of the left hand. I remember his emphasizing the use of tenths in the bass, for example. And he used to tell me that a piano man without a left hand is a very weak pianist."[8] Traditionally, of course, the two hands in jazz piano playing performed separate functions: the left provided the rhythmic drive and harmonic framework and the right outlined the melody and improvised on it. Waller, however, did not restrict melodic statements in his playing to the treble range of the piano (and hence to the right hand). Indeed, his own commentary on playing stride lays stress not on the function of an individual hand, but on a musical concept: melody. "It is my contention, and always has been, that the thing that makes a tune click is the melody, and give the public four bars of that to dig their teeth into, and you have a killer-diller. . . . And it's melody that gives variety to the ear."[9] In another context, reacting to his own rendition of Art Tatum's arrangement of "Tea for Two," Waller said:

That's music, subdued and not blatant. None of this boogie-woogie stuff that's just monotonous. Boogie-woogie is all right if you want to beat your brains out for five minutes. But for more than that you got to have melody. Jimmie Johnson taught me that. You got to hang onto the melody and never let it get boresome.[10]

Seen in this light, Maurice Waller's report of his father's assertion that "a piano man without a left hand is a very weak pianist" takes on a broader meaning. Waller's point here is that the two hands should be equally well equipped for improvisation in terms of their technical training, and that a pianist must be as capable of creating melodic invention with his left hand as with his right. Perhaps he learned these principles in his purported studies with pianist Leopold Godowsky in 1925; in any event, Waller was the first stride pianist of his generation to use his left hand for a more compelling aesthetic purpose than pumping out rhythm and harmony.[11] Of course, he couldn't simply eliminate the need for those two primary elements of the style. But by curtailing his use of stride patterns—perhaps following James P. Johnson's example—Waller was able to incorporate a substantial amount of melodic material into what his left hand played. Ironically, Waller's experience playing pipe organ, for the very same reason that it had limited his practice with stride patterns, may have enhanced his ability to use his left hand more flexibly. Freed from the obligation of striding constantly on the organ keyboard, Waller could explore the use of other, less rigidly proscribed musical gestures with his left hand.

Nevertheless, the majority of melodic activity in the early recordings is centered in the upper register of the piano. In a slow piece, Waller usually plays the melody simply, without much ornamentation. At a faster tempo, however, he uses a wide variety of technically dazzling "tricks" to embellish the melodic line. And when he improvises, he extends these gestures into long, virtuosic displays, as in the final chorus of "Numb Fumblin'," during which his right hand maneuvers through difficult passages with delicacy and deceptive ease. The tricks themselves are usually simply constructed (Example 2.2a, 2b, 2c); it's the speed of attack and absolute evenness of execution that produce the display. Waller's long, supple fingers aided him greatly in developing this flawless technique. His hands were extremely large: Richard Hadlock reports that "blind pianist George Shearing once described the experience of shaking hands with Waller as 'like grabbing a bunch of bananas.'"[12] So it is not surprising that, like any genuine virtuoso, Waller could play long passages of complicated figuration with seemingly effortless fluency. But there is a danger inherent in repeating a single gesture over several measures—that of losing the listeners' interest in the progress of the phrase. To avoid this danger, Waller varies his gestures in irregular ways or builds syncopation into them. By repeating consecutively a figure of irregular length, as in Example 2.2c, Waller can ignore the barline and upset the normal pattern of strong and weak beats. Thus, he adds an element of rhythmic tension to an otherwise potentially static series of figures.

Example 2.2a

Example 2.2b

Example 2.2c

Waller as Soloist (1929)

Waller's experiences as an apprentice of stride constituted steps in his professional education that he consciously and singlemindedly directed toward the goal of becoming a professional jazz musician. This was as true of the formal pedagogical studies he undertook as it was of his frequent informal contacts with other musicians during these years; both shaped his compositions and performances. As an apprenticeship, however, this stage in his career lasted only a few years. By the mid-1920s, Waller's recorded performances were both more effusive and swinging, and less directly inherited from ragtime than Johnson's; by the end of the decade, he was master of his own thoroughly idiosyncratic and progressive style.

This new stride style first appears in a tantalizingly brief solo from "The Henderson Stomp" (Fletcher Henderson) recorded 3 November 1926 with Fletcher Henderson and His Orchestra (matrix no. 142902-2). We can already hear unmistakable evidence of Waller's swinging, striding left hand. Yet even though the solo lasts only sixteen measures, Waller has enough time to break the stride pattern for a few beats, rattling off a series of ascending parallel tenths in its place. There is also a characteristic descending gesture in the right hand (Example 2.3), which answers the upward surge of the opening four measures of the solo.

Example 2.3

Even the individual right-hand chords in the solo's closing phrase, articulated on strong beats with a crisp, forceful attack, provide a rhythmic punch rarely found in much of his previous recorded material. On the other hand, Waller is not entirely in command of his newly acquired powers on this recording, either; his playing, especially in the left hand, is not yet as clean and error free as it would become in later sessions. It is in the solo organ recordings of 1927 (see chapter 3) and the solo piano recordings of 1929 that the stride style of Waller's first maturity finds its fullest expression.

"Numb Fumblin'" and "The Minor Drag"

Waller recorded "Numb Fumblin'," (matrix no. 49762-2) a blues of his own composition, on 1 March 1929, in Victor's New York studios. Although the unusually catchy title suggests an entirely improvisatory approach to the blues—as if Waller had composed the piece almost haphazardly, while "fumblin'" at the keyboard—in fact, he exerts a surprisingly high degree of control over the musical material. Technically, too, his performance is anything but "numb." On a superficial level, Waller constructs each of the six twelve-bar blues choruses around a single gesture or idea, which he repeats, extends, and develops through the length of the chorus. But on a more fundamental plane, these diverse-sounding choruses are unified not only through the standard blues phraseology and harmonic progressions they share, but also by the consistent reappearance of a particular motive—a rudimentary but quite effective kind of linkage that Waller was to exploit more fully in his later compositions and improvisations.

"Numb Fumblin'" consists of a brief, four-measure introduction followed by the blues choruses themselves; a two-measure tag grafted onto the final phrase of the sixth chorus concludes the piece. The first chorus begins with a single riff figure repeated over one of Waller's characteristic substitutes for the stride bass pattern—individual, left-hand chords for each beat of the measure. But in a surprising improvisational twist, Waller institutes a far-ranging harmonic progression in the third and fourth measures of the chorus. Instead of extending the tonic chord (G major) through this latter half of the phrase, which would be the usual procedure at this juncture, Waller moves by quarter notes through a series of chord changes that rapidly distance the music from its tonal center: G–F^7–Bb^7–Eb–D–B–E minor–G$^{6/4}$(i.e., V)–C^9. But this harmonic journey is circular; Waller arrives at the expected goal—a dominant chord on G—just in time to use it as preparation for the subdominant harmony of the next phrase (C major). The effect of the passage is briefly unsettling, as if Waller's keyboard fumbling had resulted in a random and meandering sequence of chords. His smooth reentry into the normal blues pattern, however, clears up the momentary sense of dislocation and effectively dispels the tension created by the unexpected progression.

Already, then, within the first eight measures of the piece, Waller has made a significant improvisational gesture. In addition, although we are unaware of it at this point, he has articulated a motive that will reappear in various shapes and contexts throughout the piece. The brief figure that constitutes the motive first appears in measure five, and is thereafter repeated several times; it consists of the outline of the interval of a rising third, B-natural to D, decorated by the preparatory grace notes A and Bb (Example 2.4a). Waller employs this same figure in the opening four-measure phrase of the second chorus accompanied there by a bass almost identical to that of the first chorus. In the following phrase, Waller turns the motive upside down, varying its original shape slightly and adding a few pitches, and he alters its rhythmic profile (Example 2.4b, m. 21). (This gesture is preceded

Example 2.4a

Example 2.4b

by a right-hand trill of two measures' duration, as evenly and flawlessly executed as any other virtuoso's would have been.) He repeats the motive throughout the second phrase and again at the close of the third four-measure phrase. For the next blues chorus, Waller creates a sharply articulated bass in which the left hand, playing in octaves, alternates between the tonic pitch (G) on strong beats and the dominant (D) on weak beats. His pointed percussive attack coupled with the substitution in the right hand of offbeat chords for melodic material lend this chorus an entirely new character, more forceful and energetic than its predecessors. But the motivic linkage to the first two choruses remains intact: Waller decorates the end of each two-measure group with a brief quotation of the motive (Example 2.4c, mm. 29–30). In the fourth chorus, Waller outlines a melodic idea in parallel thirds, beginning, after an evenly executed trill in thirds, with the inverted form of the motive from measure 21. He also incorporates the motive into a lengthy and compelling virtuoso passage in thirty-second notes comprising virtually the entire sixth chorus. Here, Waller's technique shines; the passage unfolds delicately and evenly, with just an occasional accent used to emphasize important pitches.

Example 2.4c

There are several other appearances of the motive as well, but perhaps enough evidence has already been cited to justify the assertion that a remarkable degree of cohesion exists among the melodic ideas Waller uses in each of the blues choruses. It is possible, of course, that this cohesion develops accidentally. One could argue, for example, that all the melodic figures Waller outlines lie easily under the hand and he could quickly train his fingers to play them accurately. Thus, these figures will appear more frequently than melodic shapes less immediately playable. But even if the recurring motive of "Numb Fumblin'" does constitute an easily articulated gesture (and not all of the gestures in Waller's repertoire were necessarily uncomplicated), Waller's spontaneous variations and elaborations amount to genuine development, a process no different from that initiated in eighteenth-century sonata form. Not only is the language of "Numb Fumblin'" consistent, but it is economical as well: Waller seeks to generate subsequent musical material for his improvisational passages from the few germinal ideas stated early in the piece.

Waller supplements his use of the stride bass pattern in "Numb Fumblin'" with a variety of other patterns that supply the required harmonic substructure. In "The Minor Drag" (matrix no. 49760-2), however, another of his own compositions recorded (with a small ensemble) at the same session as "Numb Fumblin'," he almost never departs from the traditional stride bass. The stride pattern works well in this setting because the group he was recording with included neither string bass nor drums; hence, the piano's function as a rhythm instrument was paramount. Waller's consistent accentuation of the first and third beats of every measure provides the rhythmic framework that keeps the group together. His striding left hand even pervades the two sixteen-measure choruses given over to his solo. Here, however, Waller employs a highly syncopated stride pattern in the first of these choruses, throwing it into prominent relief by shifting the left hand up an octave to the central register of the piano. The piano's timbre is more focused and bright here than in the bass region, where Waller has hitherto maintained the stride pattern. This sudden shift in register coupled with the frequent syncopation increases the tension and energy already inherent in the piano's percussive sound. In this new rhythmic configuration, Waller disrupts the normal pattern of accents by substituting a bass note for a tenor chord on several different weak (second and fourth) beats, increasing the frequency of this disruption as the phrase progresses. The result is not only syncopated, it is also unpredictable. Waller learned the idea from James P. Johnson; Johnson's earliest recording of "Carolina Shout" (18 October 1921) contains a passage in which he sets up a similar sequence of syncopations. Waller's pattern of displaced bass notes is not an exact duplication of Johnson's, of course, but the procedure is clearly identical.

Against this unstable bass Waller creates still further syncopation in the right hand, offsetting by approximately an eighth note what would otherwise have been a straightforward series of quarter notes. Obviously, some relief from the mounting rhythmic tension is called for, and in the second solo chorus, Waller reverts to a standard stride bass pattern, dissipating some of the pent-up energy. The key change from C minor to its relative major, E♭, also helps inaugurate a more expansive mood. Still, Waller maintains a degree of syncopation in the right hand in this chorus, playing repeated off-beat chords, which suggest the type of riff figure usually given to brass or saxes in a typical swing band arrangement. Indeed, as shortly becomes apparent, Waller introduced the figure into his solo in order to prepare for the following ensemble chorus, where the trumpet and the trombone repeat the right-hand material almost exactly as Waller had originally outlined it.

As these recordings demonstrate, then, Waller's early reputation as an accomplished stride pianist as well as a talented composer and improviser was well deserved. But by this time (1929), he had already begun to outdistance those few contemporaries who could still number themselves among his peers. His consummate technical command of the keyboard enabled him to explore an unusually broad range of expressive possibilities, of course, but he also appears to have extended himself in terms of his compositional efforts. This assertion contradicts the more commonly held view that Waller did not take his composing and performing very seriously. But the 1929 recordings, especially those from the 2 August session, leave little doubt that Waller was developing an increasingly sophisticated and subtle language; it is difficult to believe that he himself remained unaware of such progress.

"Gladyse"

The latter part of 1929 was an exceptionally busy time for Waller in terms of his recording activity. From August through December he was in the studio on no fewer than thirteen occasions, recording a total of thirty-three titles, many of them twice. These sessions comprised every conceivable kind of situation for a pianist: Waller performed solo, as an accompanist, in his own groups, and as a member of three other ensembles. But it is the piano solos that stand out from this flurry of activity as the most complete expressions of Waller's art at this stage of his career. His composition "Gladyse," a piano solo he recorded twice on 2 August 1929 (matrix nos. 49496-1 and 49496-2), is an appropriate place to begin a more detailed study of his new level of mastery in both composition and performance.

The phrase and chorus structure of "Gladyse," although unusual in its combination of different chorus types, is cast in a symmetrical and straightforward tripartite form (Figure 2.1): a sixteen-measure chorus, repeated and slightly varied (A, A'), a standard thirty-two-measure chorus, repeated and varied (B, B'), two statements of the sixteen-measure chorus (A, A"), and a brief coda. In addition to the separate structural and harmonic plans that define the two choruses, there are also some basic rhythmic and melodic distinctions between them. Chorus A is propelled by individual chords on each quarter note in the left hand (the same pattern that appears in "Numb Fumblin'"); the motivic material for the right hand consists primarily of repetitions of a short descending gesture. In chorus B Waller uses a stride bass underneath a melodic figure in the right hand outlined in parallel fourths. But he integrates this seemingly disparate material in an ingeniously simple and effective fashion. One musical link between the two choruses is embodied in the interval of a perfect fourth that is prevalent in the melodic material of both choruses. Another link involves the combination of basic right and left hand material from each chorus. In B', Waller mixes a version of the right hand motivic gesture outlined in A with the left-hand stride bass of B. But while forging this link between the two choruses, he changes the harmonic pattern supporting the combined material. Where in chorus B (mm. 39–70), Waller alternated between two harmonies (G major and C major chords) in

Figure 2.1. "Gladyse" Phrase and Chorus Structure

Section	Measure Numbers		Number of Measures
Introduction (X):	mm.	1–2	2
Chorus A:	mm.	3–18	16*
A':	mm.	19–34	16
Transition:	mm.	35–38	4
Chorus B:	mm.	39–70	32**
B':	mm.	71–102	32
(X):	mm.	103–4	2
Chorus A:	mm.	105–20	16
A":	mm.	121–36	16
Coda:	mm.	137–40	4

*Four 4-measure phrases, in an a-a-b-a pattern.
**Four 8-measure phrases, in an a-a-b-a pattern; the third phrase, or "bridge," contains new material.

two measure units, in B′ (mm. 71–102), he shifts to harmonic movement in units of one measure. This increase in the pace of harmonic motion heightens the intensity of the passage. (For some reason, Waller abandoned this important shift in the second take of "Gladyse." Instead, he uses harmonic units of one measure throughout both chorus B and B′. This difference between the two takes makes for an instructive comparison: Waller's second, more homogenized version results in a less compelling performance.)

The following statement of chorus A (mm. 105–20) essentially constitutes a recapitulation of the first appearance of this material (mm. 3–18). But in the final version of the chorus (A″, mm. 121–36), Waller again combines melodic and accompaniment material from both A and B, as he did in B′. But here, the harmonic framework derives from A instead of from B, as before. And although Waller maintains the motivic material of A, he substitutes the stride bass of B for the individual quarter-note chords of A. This reinterpretation of chorus A in the stride context of B provides a swinging and effective reworking of the original opening material. Still, Waller has not yet reached a point of repose in this piece; he appends a brief four-measure coda that gently recalls the opening chorus A material in its original format (mm. 3–18). By returning to the quarter-note chord pattern in the left hand, Waller invokes the tranquil atmosphere of the opening, and successfully dissipates the boisterous energy of the final stride chorus—a second moment, then, of genuine recapitulation.

"I've Got a Feeling I'm Falling"

Like those for "Gladyse," many of the alternate takes of the solos recorded in the latter part of 1929 have survived.[13] Starting in 1972, the French subsidiary of RCA began to reissue as much of Waller's complete recorded oeuvre as could be unearthed, including alternate takes.[14] Examining these hitherto unissued takes in conjunction with the released versions of the same songs enables us both to establish the crucial elements of Waller's style at this stage of his career and to investigate the nature and role of improvisation in his playing. Through a comparison of different takes of the same piece, it becomes possible to distinguish those stylistic and technical elements that remain constant from those that Waller varied from one performance to the next. For some stride players, improvisation consists less of sweeping revisions than of subtle changes in rhythmic accentuation, melodic ornamentation, and figuration. Waller's recorded performances, however, reveal a broad spectrum of alterations, ranging from minute changes in the pitches of the off-beat chords in the left hand to the complete overhaul of an entire thirty-two-bar chorus.

The three takes of Waller's "I've Got a Feeling I'm Falling" (matrix nos.

49494-1, 49494-2, 49494-3) provide an extensive case for investigation. In essence, we can discern three broad categories of variation among the three versions. The first category involves outright alteration—i.e., recomposition—of a passage. The basic phrase length and the general harmonic thrust of the passage, however, remain constant. Measures 29–36 offer one example of such recomposition. In take one (Example 2.5), Waller maintains the stride bass pattern throughout and adheres to an unornamented and rel-

Example 2.5

atively uncomplicated rendition of the melodic line and cadence phrase. In take two, however (Example 2.6), he eliminates the stride bass completely. He further uses miniature contrapuntal lines to enrich the texture of measures 30 and 32–34, and provides a startling harmonic conclusion (m. 35) where one would expect the simple alternation between tonic (E♭) and subdominant (A♭) of take one. Thus, in the second version, Waller takes some improvisational risks, especially in terms of both breaking up the otherwise repetitive stride bass pattern and providing unusual harmonic and accompaniment alternatives, but the risks pay off because he achieves a more sophisticated and imaginative statement of the phrase.

A second method used by Waller to alter a passage is to refine an idea already present in an earlier take. This technique involves, among other kinds of alterations, decorating a melodic line with different ornamental gestures. For example, Waller improvises on the first eight-measure phrase of the chorus in take one by playing an obbligato line high in the piano's upper register (mm. 53–60). He retains this same basic improvisation for takes two and three, but embellishes it in varying degrees. In take one, mordentlike gestures appear in the fourth and sixth measures, and the phrase concludes

Example 2.6

with a highly decorated descending figure in the seventh and eighth measures. In take two, the version eventually issued by Victor, Waller provides the same phrases with a significantly greater amount of ornamentation than that found in take one: the second, fourth, fifth, seventh, and eighth measures all bristle with delicate filigree turns and mordents. But the basic shape of the phrase remains otherwise unaltered from take one, including Waller's repetition of the closing descending figure. In the second take, then, Waller retains the same musical material he had originally improvised during the first take, but he embellishes it afresh. Finally, in take three, Waller refines the obbligato line still further: he uses melodic ornaments in the second, fourth, fifth, and sixth measures of the phrase, but substitutes a simple off-beat chordal figure for the descending line of the final two measures.

In the process of refining a particular passage in successive takes, Waller, in addition to changing melodic ornamentation, makes subtle shifts in rhythmic patterns and accentuation; he also may alter the left-hand accompaniment while retaining material for the right hand intact. The final two measures of the first eight-measure phrase of "I've Got a Feeling I'm Falling" (mm. 11–12) include a brief decorative phrase outlined in a consistently dotted rhythmic pattern. In take one, Waller uses a standard stride bass in the left hand for these measures; in take two, however, he provides a less insistent accompaniment, one more appropriate to the delicate line above it (Example 2.7a, 2.7b). At the same time, this new accompaniment gently hints at the original stride bass. Waller places the low note of the pattern prominently on the strong beat (although, of course, in take two this pitch is in the tenor range), and complements this low note with the pitches of a broken chord, placed rhythmically so that we hear two parallel descending lines, a tenth apart:

$$\left[\begin{matrix} Bb \\ G \end{matrix}\right. - \left[\begin{matrix} A \\ F\# \end{matrix}\right. - \left[\begin{matrix} Ab \\ F \end{matrix}\right.$$

Thus, this alteration for the second take provides a needed lightening of the texture and also offers momentary relief from the left hand's purposeful and jaunty stride.

A third procedure that Waller employed to vary a passage from one take to the next may be termed expansion, in which he lengthens an idea or gesture in subsequent takes. This process can be distinguished from the two described previously by the simple fact that Waller stretches the phrase by adding music to it, thus changing its shape. Expansion could clearly be applied to any section of a piece, but in the three takes of "I've Got a Feeling I'm Falling," Waller restricts its use to the introduction and coda. The intro-

Example 2.7a

Example 2.7b

ductions for takes one and two, even though they present quite different melodic and harmonic material, are both four measures long. The introduction to take three, on the other hand, lasts six measures. Waller begins with a two-measure descending figure almost identical to that of take one, but he continues by shifting to a new and unexpected harmony (*b*VI, i.e., C*b* major) for the next two measures, literally marking time with the right hand. He completes this version of the introduction in measures 5–6, first returning to the tonic and the opening figure, then moving to the dominant seventh chord underneath a similar form of the same figure.

    The codas to the three takes, examined consecutively, show an even more marked expansion. In each case, Waller alters the close of the final section harmonically in order to prepare for the additional measures of the codas. In take one, this harmonic twist appears within the final eight-measure phrase—in its fifth measure; Waller then simply grafts the two measures of coda material onto the end of the phrase. The concluding section of take one (the final phrase plus the coda) thus lasts a total of ten measures. In take two, Waller proceeds through the closing eight-measure phrase, throwing in a deceptive resolution at the last moment in the eighth measure and repeating thereafter the seventh and eighth measures. He ends this addition with two measures of the tonic pitch alone, deep in the bass register,

struck repeatedly on the offbeat. The concluding section of take two, therefore, is twelve measures long. In take three, the harmonic sequence in the
eighth measure of the final phrase incorporates a move to the minor subdominant (F minor); this shift enables Waller to add an additional six measures of
stride before coming to a truly definitive cadence. Waller's conclusion here
extends the improvisation in an effortless but unpredictable way, almost as if
he were going to continue for some time.

Waller incorporates numerous other changes into each successive performance: there are, apparently, no aspects of a piece that cannot be sub-
jected to some form of alteration—structure, transitional passages, tempi,
and so on. The passages we have examined in detail above do not involve
especially obscure variations from one take to the next; on the contrary,
most of them are quite self-evident. But these comparisons, which could not
have been made without access to the unissued takes, clarify a number of
aspects both of Waller's performance practices as a soloist on the piano and
of his composing, at the time when he first achieved the easy mastery characteristic of his style. First, he draws on a repertory of gestures and musical
ideas for expressive purposes, and he continually applies these gestures
flexibly, in different ways and in a variety of situations. For example, even
though Waller will follow a given harmonic plan for an opening chorus, he
embellishes the statement of the theme with all kinds of ornamentation. Second, he improvises frequently and substantially—that is, he creates genuinely spontaneous elaborations on a set piece of material during his
performance. The extensive and unexpected changes noted in Examples 2.6
and 2.7 (the surprise harmonic conclusion, the discarding of the stride bass)
can be accounted for in no other way. Third, the process of making several
takes of one piece for a recording permits Waller to refine or expand ideas
that may have been improvisational in the first place: he could attempt to
improve on an idea once inserted into the fabric of the work, just as a composer might undertake a revision after hearing a work's first performance.[15]

"Ain't Misbehavin'"

We need not always rely on comparisons among alternate takes of a song to
reveal the extent and the organic nature of Waller's improvisations. Some
performances demonstrate in and of themselves, without reference to other,
parallel performances, the extraordinary fertility of Waller's creations. "Ain't
Misbehavin'," arguably one of his two most popular and well-known songs
(the other is "Honeysuckle Rose"), was composed for the 1929 revue "Hot
Chocolates," which Waller wrote in collaboration with lyricist Andy Razaf.
There seem to be several different stories describing the circumstances un-

der which the song was written; the most apocryphal of them has Waller composing the music while serving his brief jail sentence for failure to pay alimony.[16] Whatever the truth of the matter, the song is a genuine masterpiece and remains as popular and widely performed today by both jazz and popular musicians as it was in Waller's lifetime.[17] Between 1930 and 1942 alone, forty recordings of the song were made by artists with styles as diverse as Louis Armstrong, Paul Whiteman, Jelly Roll Morton, and Teddy Wilson. Such statistics testify to the song's acceptance as a "standard" by jazz musicians and provide as well a broad indicator of its commercial appeal. Producers would hardly have been inclined to record it so often if substantial profits from its sales were not assured. Indeed, its success as a recording probably reflects an equal or greater popularity in terms of radio and nightclub performances.

Certainly part of its appeal derives from its artfully constructed melody—sophisticated, yet simple and memorable at the same time. Waller uses the opening gesture as a motivic cell, which he develops in subsequent measures. Both the shape and the rhythmic profile of the gesture are important because they determine how the climactic high note of the phrase is made to coincide with a strong downbeat. The motive begins with the tonic pitch (C) struck off the beat, and leaps up a fifth, landing on G on the third beat of the measure. This renders the latter half of the gesture more prominent than its opening. In the next measure (m. 2), Waller repeats the gesture beginning on D, up a whole step from the previous statement. He then states it a third time (m. 3), beginning still higher on G and adjusting its shape in consequence to conform to the new harmonic progression (i.e., the interval leap in the motive becomes a fourth instead of a fifth, ending with C, the tonic). Thus far, then, the accented pitches of each gesture (G–A–C) form a steadily rising curve articulated on the third beat of each measure. Suddenly at this point Waller increases the pace of melodic action; instead of continuing the pattern he established in the first three measures—that is, waiting to restate the motive until after the downbeat of the next measure—Waller anticipates his pattern by half a measure. He retains the most essential element of the motive—the interval leap—but compacts it to a minor third and places it over the bar line. Thus the climax of the rising line of accented pitches (G–A–C–*D*) coincides for the first time in the phrase with the downbeat, the strongest and most prominent beat of the measure. Now Waller releases the tension with a line that rapidly descends an octave, rounding out the first four measures of the eight-measure phrase. The second group of four measures begins with a repetition of the opening two, rather than a further development of the motive, and extends the final pitch of the line (m.

7, E). Finally, the entire contour of this melodic curve is underscored in the left hand by a series of rolled tenths that rise and fall in a line parallel to that of the right hand's accented pitches. [18] By rolling the tenths Waller can antici-pate the beat slightly with the lower pitch of the chord, striking the upper pitch directly on the beat and thereby strengthening its accent. In addition, when the right-hand melodic line starts to rise again in measures 5–6, the accented tenths in the left hand counteract this motion by continuing their descent, pulling the phrase back down to its point of origin and repose.

Such close analysis of a single phrase is useful up to a point in that it serves to demonstrate Waller's gift for melodic invention. What we take for granted as merely a pretty tune is actually a carefully crafted melodic line, logical and organic in its use of a motivic cell. In fact, this type of melody is characteristic of Waller's approach to the composition of a line. His predilection for short gestures that accumulate, as opposed to a long flowing line, derives from his training in stride, which stresses the need for maintaining a readily available vocabulary of short right-hand gestures for use in improvisation. Pieces as diverse as "Honeysuckle Rose," "Rusty Pail," and "(What Did I Do to Be So) Black and Blue?" all share this characteristic.

Having established the construction of the basic tune itself, we now need to examine Waller's use of this framework as a vehicle for improvisation. For example, one aspect of the opening motive's rhythm—its syncopated pro-file—informs Waller's subsequent elaborations on the tune in the piano solo version of "Ain't Misbehavin'," recorded on 2 August 1929 (matrix no. 49492-3). That is, Waller substitutes various patterns of offbeat chords for the motivic cell, gradually increasing the number of substitutions as the per-formance progresses and eliminating references to the original tune until, instead of a melodic line in the final chorus, he plays a series of abstract, isolated chords. Thus, he outlines a fairly straightforward version of the mel-ody in the first chorus; in the second chorus, he substitutes offbeat chords for approximately three measures of melody in the first phrase and for about five measures in the second; and in the third and final chorus, each phrase consists almost exclusively of the offbeat chord formulation. In fact, in the final phrase Waller even abandons the contour of the original line, preferring instead to alternate between the upper and central registers of the piano for each individual chord. The result is striking, and bears almost no resem-blance to the melody of "Ain't Misbehavin'." Yet Waller arrives at the mate-rial for this final phrase by a process of gradual substitution; the relationship of the substituted material to the original is therefore an organic one. Waller has based this improvisation on the continuous development of one aspect of his original motive, and the process of implementing the changes in the music is as orderly and logical as if the resulting music had been composed in advance. But it wasn't: Waller's genuis as an improviser lies in the fact that such development was undoubtedly the effect of spontaneous creation.

As in the case of "I've Got a Feeling I'm Falling," Waller alters the overall structure of "Ain't Misbehavin'" in this performance, adding new material at unexpected places. (Of course, Waller can only incorporate this kind of improvisation when he plays solo; in an ensemble situation, phrase length and chord progressions need to remain fixed in order to achieve coherent performances.) This flexibility tends to blur the otherwise clear-cut divisions of the Tin Pan Alley formula; by tinkering with the predictable outlines of a song's shape, however, Waller makes the transitions from one phrase or chorus to the next more fluid. Furthermore, each instance in which our expectations about a song's structure are upset forces us to listen more closely in order to discern the musical goal Waller is headed for. For example, in the last phrase of the second chorus, Waller converts the final two measures into a vehicle for a deceptive cadence, and then adds two measures to facilitate the modulation from C major, the tonic key of the piece up to this point, to E*b* major, the key for the final chorus. The additional measures thus not only prepare the new key and enable Waller to leave the melodic line of the previous phrase intact, they also give the listener adequate time to adjust to the key change. Later, Waller again uses the final two measures of a chorus— the third—to make a transition to new material, but accomplishes it here with even greater efficiency. He introduces a figure whose harmonic function is to complete (and then to repeat) the cadence of the preceding phrase, but whose motivic material anticipates in its rhythmic pattern and melodic shape that of the following phrase. There is a cleverly designed overlap here: the left hand completes one phrase while the right prepares for new material. Waller thus constructs a smooth and effective transition without requiring the addition of extra measures.

Finally, concerning this 1929 performance, we should note that Waller's prodigious command of dynamics, touch (the ability to regulate the force of his attack), and pedaling enable him to provide each phrase of "Ain't Misbehavin'" with its own distinct shading. In the bridge of the first chorus he augments a crescendo in the first four measures both with an increasingly energetic and sharp attack and through the use of the sustaining pedal; in the last four measures, his touch suddenly becomes light and gentle without losing its rhythmic drive, he stops using the sustaining pedal, and he lowers the dynamic level to *piano*. This sharp contrast is not inherent in the material (although it is probably impossible to hear it any other way once one has listened to Waller's interpretation). Rather it is Waller's characterization—

forceful for the first half, spare and delicate for the second—that separates the phrase into two balanced, juxtaposed units.

Waller's improvisations, then, are spontaneous but purposeful, and in his 1929 solo piano recordings he demonstrates his first maturity as a performer and composer. Of course, he was as adept as an accompanist for singers or in ensembles, both large and small, as he was as a soloist. The sheer quantity of recorded output in these diverse group situations as well as the variety of instruments he played—piano, celeste, pipe organ, electric organ—distinguishes him from the majority of other stride players. (Stride developed as a soloist's specialty, and it is one of Waller's contributions to the genre that he adapted it to a wide variety of performance situations. Even his contemporaries on the piano tended to specialize in just one milieu: Art Tatum and Cliff Jackson recorded primarily as soloists; Count Basie and Duke Ellington almost always appeared with their bands. Only Teddy Wilson and Earl "Fatha'" Hines seem to have proven as versatile as Waller.) Still, the solo recordings from the latter part of 1929 epitomize Waller's early style. Although rooted in the technical dexterity and standard decorative patterns of traditional stride, that style already incorporates a new and more flexible approach to harmony, structure, rhythm, and the use of the left hand, and demonstrates an organic development of motivic ideas within the course of an improvisation. It is unfortunate that Waller was never again given the opportunity to record extensively for solo piano; the few solo recordings he made after 1934 and his brief solos from the ensemble sides of the later years indicate that both his technical command of the instrument and his fund of improvisatory ideas continued to increase throughout the course of his career.

Waller as Accompanist

Although Waller recorded fewer and fewer solo sides, he remained very much in demand as an accompanist and an ensemble pianist both for recordings and for live performances. Between 1929 and 1932 he played in large ensembles with artists such as Benny Goodman and Coleman Hawkins (in a group whimsically called McKenzie's Mound City Blue Blowers), Jack Teagarden, and Ted Lewis, among others; he played in the Little Chocolate Dandies, a small pick-up group formed for only one recording session; and he recorded duets with pianist Bennie Paine (or Payne). Waller's services were even in demand by the white crooner Gene Austin for two sessions in 1929. On the first of these occasions (26 June 1929), the members of the white ensemble that accompanied Austin apparently refused to record with Waller because of his race. Austin, to his credit, insisted that Waller be permitted to play. Eventually, an agreement between Austin and the white musicians (it could hardly be called a compromise) was reached that mandated a bizarre disposition of the instruments: Waller, playing piano, was segregated at one end of the recording studio while the white musicians were huddled at the other.[19] Predictably, this arrangement produced takes in which the only signs of vitality and artistry come from Waller's playing; the rest is sentimental schmaltz—a grotesque parody of the music. The recordings, then, are a minor triumph of poetic justice for Waller.

Other recorded evidence from these years reveals that Waller's style when playing in ensembles differed markedly from one session to the next. The cause of these stylistic variations is not entirely clear. It may simply have been that, like any musician, Waller was emotionally prepared for some sessions and not for others. Or perhaps he felt less inhibited (and hence more willing to take bold improvisational chances) in groups he led himself than in groups directed by others, even though groups nominally under his direction were assembled by producers for individual recording sessions. (Not until after 1934 would Waller have a longstanding association with the same group of musicians—that is, a continuous relationship with them as their leader.) At least some of Waller's group recordings in the 1930s seem to confirm this hypothesis. For example, the 10 November 1931 session in which Waller joined trombonist Jack Teagarden and His Orchestra resulted in takes of "China Boy" (matrix no. 10976-1) and "Tiger Rag" (matrix no. 10979-1) that were both rejected by Victor. Waller's playing in the ensemble as a whole and behind the individual solos in these takes is straightforward, even bland and self-effacing. He provides only the most basic rhythmic and harmonic background. The solos he contributes likewise lack any particular flair or compelling ideas. In fact, in his "China Boy" solo, Waller fails to follow the harmonic changes of the second phrase, and consequently stumbles repeatedly over a gesture whose pitches are foreign to the underlying harmony. (Perhaps this noticeable confusion was in part responsible for Victor's eventual rejection of the take.) Again, in the sides he recorded with Billy Banks and His Orchestra (under the name "The Rhythmakers") in July 1932, almost no hint of Waller's unique and engaging presence emerges. Yet the "Fats Waller and His Buddies" recordings from an 18 December 1929 session show Waller as an accomplished and thoughtful accompanist, even though the group was one assembled just for this session. In "Won't You Get off It, Please?" (matrix no. 57928-1), Waller backs the energetic trumpet solo with the simplest of countermelodies—a series of accented but slow-moving pitches in the piano's middle range. Then, to accompany the tenor sax, he switches to rifflike chords played in the high register. Thus, he uses the piano's broad range to advantage in his accompaniments, providing material that complements each of the individual solos in an appropriate way.

This kind of sensitivity to the soloist is most apparent in Waller's accompaniment of Monette Moore, a blues singer who, like Sara Martin, had recorded a number of sides in the mid-1920s. Together, Waller and Moore recorded a medley of "A Shine on Your Shoes" and "Louisiana Hayride" on 28 September 1932,[20] and their collaboration represents an interesting confluence of musical styles. Although they had not recorded together before, Waller and Moore were each well acquainted with the standard mid-1920s approach to blues recordings (female vocalist supported by piano accompaniment) since they had both made numerous such recordings. On this date, however, their material consisted of popular tunes whose musical shape and substance were derived not from the blues tradition but from the standard Tin Pan Alley chorus arrangement of four eight-measure phrases in an AABA pattern. By now, Waller had acquired extensive experience playing such arrangements in ensembles of different sizes, which had equipped him to respond to a wide variety of soloing styles. With Moore, he was free to fashion his accompaniment without reference to additional supporting instrumentation, and he became inventive as well as accomplished, creating a part that could almost stand as an improvisation on its own. In fact, Waller's playing here resembles that of an equal partner in a duet (just as his earlier pipe organ work complemented rather than merely supported the individual musicians of the Louisiana Sugar Babes, a group he recorded with in 1928).[21]

In the first chorus of "A Shine on Your Shoes" Waller's right hand remains mostly independent of the melodic line, occasionally adding a typical stride gesture, repeated above an extended vocal note at the end of a phrase, or a fragment of obbligato to complement the vocal line. When Moore improvises on the melody in the second chorus, however, Waller provides only a modest background—an unadorned stride bass; thus he avoids interfering with the singer's spontaneous elaborations. Waller's accompaniment for the second part of the medley follows a similar pattern, except that he doubles the melody in the first chorus and takes one chorus as a solo. Throughout the medley, Waller envinces a restraint and delicacy both in dynamic levels and in figuration, while simultaneously maintaining the rhythmic propulsion that makes the performance swing. The recording is an excellent example of Waller's ability to accompany another artist without submerging his own distinctive musical persona.

Waller as Singer

One other aspect of this persona, crucial both to Waller's enormous growth in popularity and to his development as a performing artist, surfaces in a few recordings made in the early 1930s: his singing. At some point late in 1929 or in 1930, Waller came under contract to the publisher and promoter Joe Davis. Davis, through Frank Walker, who was the popular music director at Columbia, arranged a session at the Columbia studios in which Waller played with a band assembled by Ted Lewis. [22] This group recorded four songs on 5 and 6 March 1931, and Waller sang on three of them: "I'm Crazy 'bout My Baby" (matrix no. 151396-1), "Dallas Blues" (matrix no. 151397-3), and "Royal Garden Blues" (matrix no. 151398-2). These are, in fact, Waller's first significant vocal performances on recordings. The producers at Columbia were apparently pleased with the results since they brought Waller back to the studio a week later (on 13 March 1931) to record "I'm Crazy 'bout My Baby" again and "Draggin' My Heart Around" as piano/vocal solos (matrix nos. 151417-3 and 151418-2, respectively). Waller was also performing at the Hotfeet Club, a nightclub in Greenwich Village, for about six months in 1931. [23] He doubtless supplemented his piano playing there with jokes, humorous asides, and probably some singing, further expanding the role of humor and satire in his act. Finally, he made recordings with two groups late in 1931 and in 1932 in which he again sang (or, more accurately, satirized the lead singer's efforts). Of those titles he recorded with Jack Teagarden and His Orchestra on 14 October 1931 two—"You Rascal, You" (matrix no. 151839-1) and "That's What I Like About You" (matrix no. 151840-1)—include vocal interpolations by Waller. He also participated as a vocalist on the two takes of "Mean Old Bed Bug Blues" (matrix nos. 12120-1, 12120-2) recorded on 26 July 1932 with the Rhythmakers.

Waller's vocal style is not, as often assumed by white critics, merely a formulaic compendium of gags, satiric thrusts, exaggerated pronunciations and phrasings, and standard tag lines added at the song's close. In fact, such a negative judgment probably reflects not a careful assessment of Waller's performances, but more a heartfelt and genuine exasperation with the supposed waste of a great talent on the trivial, pedestrian material Waller was required to record at Victor in the late 1930s (see chapter 4). For a thorough evaluation shows clearly that the obvious elements of humor he incorporates serve primarily to embellish and enliven his delivery; they do not in and of themselves constitute the essence of his wit, nor do they explain his effectiveness as a satirist. The early recordings on which he sings—i.e., those from 1931 and 1932—reveal a much more subtle approach to the lyrics of a song than Waller's critics might acknowledge. Indeed, Waller's vocal style is clearly derived from and fully consonant with the stride idiom in which he was so well versed as a pianist. His singing, in other words, embodies the same stylistic principles of improvisation as his playing—a fluent technique, a wide repertoire of preconceived gestures flexibly applied, and the use of motivic cells that undergo a process of development and alteration in the course of an improvised solo.

The most basic, and in many ways important, element of Waller's singing is the quality of his voice itself. A clear and penetrating high baritone, with little vibrato, it can pierce through the instrumental texture of any ensemble, large or small. In later recordings, Waller frequently alters the tone of his voice, either increasing its intensity by providing a gravelly edge to the sound or softening its thrust through a breathy, unfocused delivery. But in the recordings of the early 1930s, he generally retains his natural vocal quality, reinforcing its hard purity with a clipped, precise enunciation of the lyrics. Like the greatest jazz vocalists (Bessie Smith, for example[24]), Waller also had an excellent sense of pitch, phrasing, accent, timing, dynamic control, and rhythm. He used all of these tools skillfully to reshape the text according to his own interpretation, either to underscore the import of the lyrics or, more frequently, to provide an ironic or irreverent counterpoint to their meaning. He occasionally even resorted to spoken declamation of the lines for satiric purposes, too—in an exaggerated and melodramatic inflection, of course.[25]

Waller's first singing on record, the rendition of his song "I'm Crazy 'bout My Baby" made with Ted Lewis and His Band on 5 March 1931 (matrix no. 151396-1) is, with the exception of the spirituals he recorded at the end of the decade,[26] one of his least satiric and unembellished vocal performances. Nevertheless, it still reveals a high degree of sophistication in his vocal improvisation. The text and melodic line of the bridge of "I'm Crazy 'bout My Baby" (as rendered by Waller in the 5 March recording) appear in Examples 2.8a and 2.8b. In Example 2.8a, the first statement of the bridge in the 5 March version, Waller basically follows the original (i.e., composed) rhythmic and pitch patterns for each of the short phrases except the final one. There, he doubles the length of the phrase (extending it from four to eight beats) and places each syllable of the word *understand* on a strong beat. The unaltered original shape of this gesture would have paralleled that of the third and fourth measures. But Waller's rhythmic realignment of the music for these two measures, coupled with the upward shift in pitch, not only break up the recurring pattern (♩♪♪♪|♪♪♩) but also provide a more exciting climax to the bridge than the line in its original shape. The

Example 2.8a

Example 2.8b

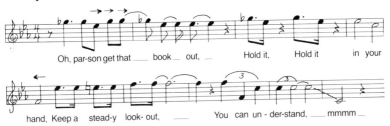

changes Waller makes for the second vocal statement of the bridge are extensive (Example 2.8b). He sings the phrase almost entirely in the upper part of his range, completely overhauling the melodic line and emending the text. Most significant, he substitutes a new and arresting rhythmic profile for the original. This new feature consists of two highly contrasting elements: syncopation (which displaces the normal pattern of accents) and strong, unambiguous downbeats (which reinforce the normal pattern of accents). Two short syncopated gestures (mm. 1–2 and 7–8), so subtly articulated that they probably cannot be notated with total accuracy, surround four measures in which Waller uses accented downbeats almost exclusively. The sharp juxtaposition of these two elements creates a nervy, unpredictable, and hence exciting rhythmic scheme. The phrase also contains one unambiguous reference to the original pattern (♩ ♫ ♩ ♪ ♩ ♫ ♩ ♩   ) in measures 5–6. In the midst of the new and vastly different material, then, Waller graciously provides his listeners with at least one comforting (albeit brief) moment anchored in familiar music.

Comparing the 5 March rendition to Waller's solo performance of "I'm Crazy 'bout My Baby" recorded the following week on 13 March 1931 further clarifies the nature and extent of his vocal improvisations on both text and melody. Waller sings the bridge phrase in this recording three times (Examples 2.8c, 2.8d, 2.8e), and again, each vocal statement provides a different interpretation of the line. In the first (2.8c) Waller merely delays very slightly each of the major downbeats (mm. 2, 4, 6, 8). This is, after all, the first time the bridge material appears in this recording, and Waller thus presents it in its most basic and unaltered form. He holds back on the downbeats simply to include a miniscule pitch ornament (the sliding descent to the F of "hand"), and to exaggerate the initial consonants of "look" and "stand."

Example 2.8c

This first chorus is followed by a second for piano solo. Then, in the third chorus, Waller sings through the lyrics again. When he comes to the bridge (Example 2.8d), he maintains the original rhythmic profile of measures 1–2 and 5–6, but interpolates repetitions of the text in measures 3, 4, and 7. These interpolations necessitate a drastically altered rhythmic pattern in order to accommodate the additional words without expanding the phrase beyond its fixed eight-measure length. Here Waller again achieves an unpredictable and jumpy rhythmic profile—perhaps an oblique commentary on the parson's inability to hold the book "steady in his hand." (Indeed, any parson faced by so large and enthusiastic a groom as Fats Waller would have had good reason to tremble.)

Example 2.8d

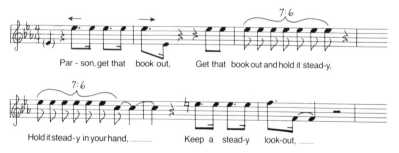

Sure-ly you can, sure-ly you can   un - der - - - stand,

As if to alleviate the tension caused by the syncopation and rhythmic complexity of this statement of the bridge, Waller adopts a simple, rifflike pattern for the bridge in the closing chorus (Example 2.8e). The first and third beats of each of the first five measures in the phrase are accented (a pattern Waller takes up for the opening gesture of the next phrase: "It's an A-one combination"). Then Waller syncopates the words ". . . look out, you can . . .," momentarily breaking up the riff. Finally, he returns to accenting individual quarter note beats in measures 7–8 before reestablishing the riff for the next phrase. Like the final chorus of a typical stride piano solo (as in the third take of "I've Got a Feeling I'm Falling," for example), Waller shifts into a "shout" or "stomp" style for the vocal line in order to provide the maximum amount of rhythmic energy and excitement for the song's final chorus.

Example 2.8e

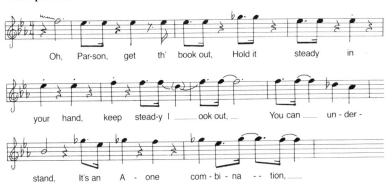

Oh, Par-son, get th' book out, Hold it steady in

your hand, keep stead-y I ____ ook out, __ You can ___ un - der -

stand, It's an A - one com - bi - na - - tion, ___

At the end of this version of the song, Waller changes the line "I'm crazy 'bout my baby, and my baby's crazy about me" to "I'm exasperated about my offspring, and my offspring's exasperated about me." It is a typically witty Waller emendation: the colloquial and contextual meaning of *baby* here is "lover," but Waller ignores that meaning and replaces the word with its literal synonym, *offspring*. The same kind of replacement process functions in the substitution of *exasperated* for *crazy*, although the two are not really synonyms. The joke results from Waller's clever reversal of the technique of punning. A pun is created by using the same word in different contexts, thereby suggesting different (and usually opposite) meanings for the word. Here, however, Waller uses two different words that actually have the same (or nearly the same) literal meaning—*baby* and *offspring*—but which acquire entirely different connotations when placed in the same context, thus reversing or drastically altering the sense of the lyric. Rather than an expression of enthusiastic passion for the singer's lover, then, Waller's substitution evokes the annoyance of a parent for a child's wayward behavior. This change in intent ridicules the whole premise of the lyric by mocking the title line itself, thus showing Waller to be an effective and penetrating satirist.[27]

In addition to this modification, Waller interpolates some pungent spoken commentary during the song's piano introduction, the piano solo chorus, and the coda. The text of the patter over the introduction and the mincing tone of Waller's delivery serve as broad cues that, like any good jazz performer, Waller will use the preexisting material to his own aesthetic ends, which, in this case, are satiric ones.

> *My* goodness, I feel so effervescent this morning
> (small sigh)
> (High pitched big sigh) Everything's so eulogizin'—
> Listen, can you stand me to tell you about it?
> Listen here: . . .

At this point, Waller starts to sing the text itself, but how are we to take the narrator's first line, "I'm walkin' on air," after hearing Waller tell us, in his mock-sophisticated tone, that he feels "effervescent"—a reference to the effects of some intoxicating substance on the singer (champagne, possibly, since it is bubbly, or perhaps something decidedly more potent)? Alex Hill, the lyricist, certainly intended this phrase as a metaphor for happiness—its commonly understood meaning—but in Waller's version, the singer comes off as definitely inebriated.

During the piano solo, Waller's spoken asides, although still satiric, also provide an allegorical context for the solo—a program, as it were, illustrated by the music. (In the following quotation of Waller's commentary, to indicate the placement of each of the spoken asides in the solo I have put the phrase designation of each of the eight-measure phrases—A–A–B–A—and the measure number within that phrase next to the appropriate line of text.)

A	m.	4	Let's waltz the rhumba!
A	m.	1	Boy, will you get off?
	m.	7	Now let's go uptown:
B	mm.	2–3	Oh, we're now floatin' down the Hudson—
	mm.	4–6	Mercy, oh you slay me, you sweet thing!
	m.	8	Oh, baby! (High pitched sigh—a duplicate of the second sigh in the introductory patter.)

The third and fourth lines bear the closest relationship to what happens in the music itself. The location "uptown" has both a literal and figurative meaning. Literally, it refers to Harlem and serves to introduce (and justify) the use of typical stride figuration for the bridge that follows immediately. For Waller, and for much of his audience, the links that connect "uptown" to Harlem, and Harlem, as the birthplace and home of stride piano, to Fats Waller, would have been self-evident. Figuratively, "uptown" suggests the upper (treble) register of the piano. Waller's speaking the word coincides with the shift of his right hand to that register for the following stride figuration. And his comment, "Oh, we're now floatin' down the Hudson" provides a pictoral frame of reference that mirrors the action of that figuration—a delicately articulated gesture in thirds, which, in spite of occasional eddys interrupting the otherwise lazy descent, meanders steadily down from the high register.

Finally, Waller's spoken lines at the song's close amount to another satiric thrust at the text's basic premise:

> Now listen, would you like to come over for a
>   cup of coffee, baby?
> Maybe. . . .

If even this mild invitation is qualified with a cool "Maybe" (or is Waller here supplying his baby's answer to the invitation?), then we are forced to wonder exactly how crazy about his baby Waller actually is (or vice versa).

Clearly, as our analyses of both the five vocal statements of the bridge phrase of "I'm Crazy 'bout My Baby" and the spoken asides demonstrate, Waller's singing at this stage of his career was anything but routine.[28] His improvisations on the original bridge phase (Examples 2.8b, 2.8d, and 2.8e) are neither mindless nor formulaic, but offer instead spontaneously conceived yet interrelated reinterpretations of text and melodic line, especially in their rhythms. In the solo version of 13 March in particular, Waller uses the preexisting textual and musical material to aesthetic ends that are as rewarding as they are satiric. It is jazz of the highest caliber, and reflects Waller's rich and fertile store of ideas. His career still had eleven highly productive years to run before his death in 1943; he continued to grow and mature through those years as a singer and pianist, despite the incredibly hectic pace of recording and concert dates he was forced to keep up. As we examine the achievements of later years in chapter 4, we will continue to find developments in his style whose origin, as we have established here, lies in the works of this, his first maturity—1929–32.

3

Born Again:
The Pipe Organ as Jazz Instrument

Waller's series of pipe organ recordings for Victor in the late 1920s constitutes a repertoire unique in the history of jazz. No other major figure made
so many jazz recordings of such consistently high quality on the pipe organ.
Given both the nominal similarity between organ and piano keyboards, and
the number of jazz pianists making records during this era, one could ask
why no strong and productive jazz tradition for the pipe organ evolved. Despite the apparent similarities, however, substantial differences do exist between the organ and the piano, differences Waller exploited. A close look at
the intrinsic nature of each instrument and at the circumstances surrounding
Waller's early efforts on the pipe organ may help illuminate both the significance of Waller's achievement and the reasons it was never duplicated.

Tone is produced on the piano when a felt hammer strikes a string; the
amount of physical force used by the pianist in depressing the key therefore
affects both the level of volume and the quality of sound. That is, the pianist
can shade his initial attack in a variety of ways, from gentle and understated
to strongly percussive, thereby gaining an impressive degree of control over
the timbre, or color of the tone. Such control assumes a crucial significance
for any performer, but especially for the black performer since black vernac-
ular music, whether from the folk, church, blues, or jazz traditions, tends to
be characterized by emotional immediacy. Clearly, the greater the degree of
control over the sound, the more closely the performer can project his emotional message or stance (i.e., attain emotional immediacy) through his
playing.

The modern pipe organ on the other hand, cannot be responsive to the
performer's will in the same direct way as the piano. An organ produces

sound when air is released into a pipe. A sophisticated electrical mechanism connects each note on the keyboard to the appropriate pipe.[1] Thus, the force used in depressing the key has no effect whatsoever on the volume or quality of the organ's tone, and the performer lacks the kind of control possible on the piano. Still, the organist has at least three basic means of varying the instrument's tone, even if they are all mechanical in nature. First, the volume can be altered (without necessarily changing the timbre) by manipulating an expression pedal (a foot pedal that operates exactly like an automobile accelerator). Second, the volume and timbre can be altered simultaneously by closing a circuit that increases the number of pitches and/or stops played from a single key on the keyboard. The third major expressive possibility consists in drawing on the variety of sound qualities and colors associated with each of the organ's dozens of stops. (A stop is a plunger or tab switch mounted, together with other similar switches, in panels or banks located at the sides of or above the organ's keyboards.) Each stop, when engaged, connects an individual keyboard to a set of pipes with a particular timbre. A string stop engages pipes that imitate the sound of strings, a flute stop, pipes that sound like flutes, and so on. The greater the number of stops available, the greater the possibilities for unusual timbres and timbral combinations. Nevertheless, the organist is still separated from the instrument's source of sound by an electrical mechanism, and it is this limitation—a lack of direct control by the fingers over the sound—that may have inhibited some jazz pianists from attempting to perform on the organ.

And in any case, practically speaking, Afro-Americans of the nineteenth and early twentieth centuries probably did not have the kind of access to large pipe organs that they did to almost every other instrument of Western European origin. Unlike the trumpet, clarinet, trombone, or guitar, for example, the pipe organ was neither portable nor inexpensive. Unlike the piano, it was not ubiquitous. And in those few churches of black congregations wealthy enough to have a pipe organ, its location in such an institution—the bastion of black middle-class respectability—kept it isolated from even the possibility of jazz performance.[2] Indeed, we know from the attitude of Waller's own parents that sacred music and jazz occupied extreme positions at opposite poles of a rigidly defined moral spectrum, whatever the historical, technical, and aesthetic ties between them.

Waller, however, because of his steady jobs at the Lincoln and Lafayette theaters, played secular music on large pipe organs regularly from about 1919 on. These positions, which required both improvisation (for silent film accompaniment) and entr'acte renditions of popular tunes (for intermissions between the acts of vaudeville shows), provided him with the opportunity to explore fully the instrument's capabilities. We should emphasize the fact that Waller received no formal instruction on the organ, in contrast to his stride piano tutelage by James P. Johnson. Thus, no particular approach or technique was impressed upon him; he remained free to devise independent or unorthodox solutions for problems in performance. In the process, he developed both an impressive technique and the means to make the organ immediately responsive to the emotional attitude he wanted to project.

By the time Waller came to make his first pipe organ recordings for the Victor Talking Machine Company in November 1926, he was already an accomplished jazz organist. The instrument he played for these sessions represented something of a hybrid between two distinct types of pipe organs: the theater organ and the standard church organ of the time. Victor had purchased the Trinity Church building located at 114 North 5th Street, in Camden, New Jersey, in the early 1920s; the company's executives had apparently been impressed with the church's excellent acoustic properties, and hence with its potential as a recording studio. In addition, the original pipe organ, built and installed in the church by the Estey Organ Company of Brattleboro, Vermont, had remained in good and playable condition. However, because Victor intended to use the new studio to record works from a wide variety of repertoires—orchestral and operatic as well as popular— major alterations in the organ's design were deemed necessary. These modifications were completed by the Estey Company during the first half of 1925; some further additions and corrections to the instrument were carried out in May 1926. A lively and detailed correspondence between G. S. Boyer, Estey's Philadelphia representative, and Col. J. G. Estey, in Brattleboro, traces the progress of both the negotiations concerning the design and purchase of the instrument and its installation in the church.[3]

When the organ renovation was finished, the new instrument (opus 2370) incorporated most of the basic characteristics of Estey's version of a standard church organ (retained from the original two-manual instrument, opus 1859) and some features usually found only on theater organs as well. (See Appendix for the final specifications of the Estey organ, opus 2370.) Second touch, for example, a device built into the organ's keyboard, was invented by a British theater organ specialist, Robert Hope-Jones. It permits the performer to add a different set of pipes to those already in use merely by depressing the keys of a particular keyboard about one-eighth of an inch beyond their usual stopping point. This action closes an electrical circuit that engages the additional pipes, instantly altering the quality of sound for the same pitch or chord without interruption of the tone. The original timbre, of course, can be just as quickly recaptured by releasing the keys. Second touch thus facilitates loud accents or rapid shifts in the quality of the sound (a capability important for a performer who, in accompanying silent movies, would need to underscore the melodramatic and often hectic progress of their plots).

Waller recorded on the Estey instrument in a variety of situations: as soloist, accompanist to singers, and member of a small group. The majority of these sessions took place between 1926 and 1929, past the years of Waller's apprenticeship, but still early in his recording career. Twenty-seven titles, or just under half the total number of pipe organ recordings, are solos, and Waller made multiple takes of complete versions of almost all of them. (Even when they were preserved, however, alternate takes were never issued contemporaneously with the released take, and a few titles were simply rejected outright by the producer.) He recorded a total of eighteen titles with different ensembles; again, some of these were not issued. Finally, Waller provided pipe organ accompaniment for singers other than himself on nine titles, and accompanied his own singing in solo sessions on just six titles. The majority of all of these pieces were recorded by Victor at its Camden studio. But Waller recorded a small number of sides during his 1938 and 1939 London tours. On these occasions he played the Compton organ (a bona fide theater organ) in the Abbey Road studios of His Master's Voice company (HMV). He recorded solos, accompanied his own singing and that of Adelaide Hall, and played with a small ensemble.[4]

The central problem confronting Waller in creating viable jazz performances on the pipe organ was how to make this cumbersome and grandiose instrument swing. Swing results from a variety of factors in performance, among them rhythmic propulsion and precision. In jazz of this period, the piano can and ordinarily does function as a rhythm instrument; making it swing poses no intrinsic problem to the skilled performer. The percussive snap that initiates the piano's sound when the hammer strikes the key helps to articulate a clear and precise beat, and the accents a performer may place on any individual pitch or chord animate the driving, energetic left-hand patterns which are the essence of stride.[5] But the organ keyboard, as we saw, does not respond to the force of the player's touch, nor is there any percussive element in the creation of tone in an organ pipe.

Waller's recordings reveal an effective solution to this problem. In general, he uses the pedalboard—the keyboard played by the feet—to provide the underlying fundamental pitches of a given harmony on the first and third beats of a 4/4 (common time) measure. This pattern isolates the strong beats of a measure, thereby fostering the illusion that they have been accented. (On the piano, rolled tenth chords—

—usually occur on the strong beats of a measure, but such chords, because they contain three widely spaced pitches, could not be played on an organ pedalboard in the space of one quarter-note beat by even the most agile and long-legged performer.) In conjunction with these bass notes, Waller plays chords with his left hand either on the weak beats of a 4/4 measure or on all four beats of the measure. The second of these two configurations occurs more frequently, appearing in almost all the solo pipe organ recordings made for Victor. This combination of pedal bass notes played on strong beats and tenor range chords played on all four beats, articulated by short taps that produce a sharp, clearly defined staccato, creates the forward momentum essential to swing.

Interestingly, a similar kind of configuration can occasionally be heard on piano recordings as a substitute for the normal stride pattern. The two takes of "Gladyse," recorded on 2 August 1929 (matrix no. 49496-1 and -2), both incorporate the use of four mid-range chords without a bass note on the strong beats in the opening chorus. Playing at a *piano* dynamic level, Waller uses a very delicate staccato touch to articulate the accompaniment; neither the forward momentum of the swing nor the clarity of the harmonic progression is diminished. "Gladyse," however, was composed and recorded after this kind of pattern had appeared on many of the pipe organ sides; thus it may represent an adaptation to the piano of a technique developed for the pipe organ. There is also at least one clear instance in a pipe organ recording of a device in the bass accompaniment that derives directly from stride piano practice. In the version of "Beale Street Blues" that Waller recorded with the singer Alberta Hunter on 20 May 1927 (matrix no. 38046-2), he plays a solo on the pedals (i.e., in the bass) for the fourth chorus improvisation. By interspersing left-hand chords at unexpected intervals, Waller sets up a syncopated pattern that, like that of his solo in "The Minor Drag" (see chapter 2), reflects the influence of James P. Johnson on his playing.

In addition to making the organ swing by making it rhythmically responsive, Waller takes full advantage of the pipe organ's capabilities in his treatment of the melodic line, subjecting it in his improvisations to a variety of effects not possible on the piano. Because the organ's pipes sound continuously at a steady volume, they can produce a legato line much like that of a wind instrument. (The piano's sound decays immediately after the string has been struck.) Thus, we often find Waller tracing a simple, unadorned legato melody against a more rhythmically active background, as in "Persian Rug" (matrix no. 42569-1). This same legato phrasing functions equally well in articulating a countermelody, as in "Persian Rug," where the countermelody is played simultaneously against the main melodic line in the organ, and in "When You're with Somebody Else" (matrix no. 42532-2), where it provides counterpoint to the trombone's line in the opening chorus. (A countermelody is a melodic line played simultaneously with the main melody, subsidiary to it, but nevertheless prominent and independent of it.) The organ can also produce the exact opposite of a smooth legato, as we have noted, and a melody articulated in a crisp staccato will pierce through the texture with its sharp, brittle clarity. In several solos—"St. Louis Blues" (matrix no. 36773-1), "Soothin' Syrup Stomp" (matrix no. 37357-2), "Hog Maw Stomp" (matrix no. 37820-1), and "Tanglefoot" (matrix no. 56069-1)—Waller uses this articulation for individual phrases, occasionally enriching the texture by adding chords to the melodic pitches of an entire line. In this particular configuration, each pitch of the melody retains a position as the highest pitch of a three-, four-, or five-note chord. The resulting sonority in some respects resembles that produced by Waller's articulation of riffs on the pipe organ keyboard, except that riffs—chords played in repeated rhythmic patterns—generally lack a strong melodic profile. On the few pipe organ recordings where Waller does incorporate riffs into his performances, he tends to reserve them for the concluding phrase of the final chorus, as in "The Digah's Stomp" (matrix no. 40095-2). In such cases, the riff heightens the rhythmic energy of the piece's climax (the "stomp" effect), much as a brass section might at the close of a piece for a large jazz band. Indeed, because of its reserves of sonorous power, as well as its ability to duplicate the crisp attack and cut-off of brass and wind instruments, the pipe organ is ideally suited to reproducing riffs as part of the texture of a piece.

The organ's array of stops affords Waller still another means of affecting his presentation of the melodic line. By choosing a particular registration (i.e., combination of stops), Waller can sharply differentiate the instrumental color of the line from that of the accompaniment. In fact, registration itself often becomes a significant factor in Waller's improvisation. Thus, in addition to reshaping the original melodic profile or incorporating a variety of embellishments to decorate it, Waller will in some cases provide a new registration for the line (as in the second blues chorus of the second take of "The Digah's Stomp"). The change in timbre, immersing the original musical material in a new aural context, reveals fresh qualities in the already familiar profile and structure of the line itself. In an orchestral work, a composer achieves a similar effect by placing a melodic idea first in one section of the orchestra and then in another—strings and brass, for example. Waller uses shifts in registration in other ways, as well: to distinguish a particular chorus or phrase, to emphasize call and response patterns (i.e., brief, well-defined gestures or phrases, a bar or so in length, linked together in pairs that suggest a question-and-answer rhetorical structure), and to facilitate sudden changes in dynamic level. These rapid shifts can be accomplished effortlessly since a differing registration would be selected for each keyboard on the organ; thus Waller need only play a different keyboard to produce the new sound.

This broad range of sonaural possibilities fascinated and attracted Waller. Playing the organ became for him an especially rewarding enterprise, and he preferred it to the piano. Ashton Stevens, music critic of the *Chicago American* newspaper, is supposed to have said, "The organ is the favorite instrument of Fats's heart; and the piano only of his stomach."[6] Waller himself phrased the same thought less archly than Stevens, but more to the point: "I really love the organ. I can get so much more color from it than the piano that it really sends me."[7] In any case, to understand how Waller uses the complex of diverse possibilities and devices to create powerfully swinging jazz on the pipe organ, we need to examine their appearance in the differing contexts of the pieces themselves—solo, vocal accompaniment, and ensemble.

Solo Recordings

Waller first recorded on the Estey pipe organ on 17 November 1926, both as a soloist and in an ensemble. The group with which he played on this occasion, called the Six Hot Babies, made no fewer than four takes of the spiritual "All God's Chillun Got Wings," but these were all rejected by Victor. But the pianist of the group, Nathaniel Shilkret, was Victor's Director of Light Music from 1915 to 1945, and he apparently took more than a passing interest in recording Waller at the organ. In addition to the Six Hot Babies session, Waller made a trial record on solo organ for Shilkret at his next Victor session on 14 January 1927 ("I'd Like to Call You My Sweetheart," matrix no. 37363-1), and in March 1928 he played organ in a trio and quartet put together by Shilkret to record two other popular tunes. Both of these groups were named "Shilkret's Rhyth-Melodists," and consisted of rather odd combinations of instruments for a jazz ensemble; the quartet, for example, included the harpist of the New York Philharmonic Orchestra, Francis J. Lapitino.

Another Victor producer eager to record Waller on pipe organ and piano was Ralph Peer, who had previously held the position of president of Southern Music Company, a publishing firm. Peer had overseen Waller's very first recordings, made for the Okeh label on 21 October 1922, and may have remembered the session since the record apparently sold fairly well.[8] Perhaps more significantly, Peer had been among the first to discover that recordings made by black artists would be eagerly purchased by the black community, and thus generate substantial revenue for the recording company. It was clearly not aesthetic considerations alone that prompted Peer to organize Waller's session at the Estey pipe organ; it must also have been obvious to him that Waller's ability to create genuine jazz on the instrument would result in performances of enormous appeal to the record-buying members of the black community.

On 14 January 1927 Waller recorded seven titles for Victor at its Camden studio (the session organized by Shilkret). All seven were pipe organ solos; this, then, was not a hastily conceived or impromptu session, but rather one that Shilkret had planned to take advantage of Waller's unique abilities as a jazz organist on the studio's refurbished instrument. Three takes were apparently made of each of six titles recorded on this date; the seventh was the trial record made for Shilkret,[9] and no master or copy of it survives. Of the other six titles, multiple takes of four are still available, including unissued versions: three takes of "Soothin' Syrup Stomp," two each of "Sloppy Water Blues," "Messin' Around with the Blues," and "Rusty Pail." One take of "Loveless Love" also has been preserved.

Each extant take of the five surviving titles reveals a variety of features of Waller's pipe organ playing, but "Rusty Pail" offers the most fertile ground for examination. Like the other songs recorded at this session (except for "Loveless Love"), it was composed by Waller. Its structure is not merely a blues (as suggested by Cangardel),[10] but rather a compendium of chorus types—thirty-two-bar AABA, twelve-bar blues, and independent eight-bar phrases. Furthermore, these distinctive types of structural units are linked by a high degree of motivic unity and harmonic coherence. The overall structure of the first take of "Rusty Pail" (see Figure 3.1) comprises a four-bar introduction followed by three sections, each manifesting a different internal structure; these are followed by two thirty-two-bar choruses, each a different variation on the first of the three sections. The abrupt shift from one phrase arrangement to the next in the first three sections—especially in a purely instrumental context—is an unusual feature that could, in the hands of a less skilled composer, prove unsettling to the listener. The art of improvisation, after all—and indeed, the structure of most jazz performances at this stage in jazz's history—is based on the notion that a block of pre-scribed material (i.e., the tune in its original form) will be used as the basis for a series of spontaneously composed variations which follow it. If a thirty-two-bar AABA chorus occurs at the beginning of a piece, subsequent cho-ruses, under normal circumstances, will be based on this material and will therefore share its structure. In "Rusty Pail," however, Waller inserts two twelve-bar blues choruses following the opening thirty-two-bar chorus, and he introduces further complexity by inserting thereafter an independent eight-bar phrase and repeating it. Only then does he return to the original thirty-two-bar AABA format to present two choruses of improvised varia-tions based on the material in the opening chorus.

How Waller provides continuity among this variety of chorus types—that is, how he links the opening chorus with the closing variations based on that chorus without rendering the intervening material of the blues chorus and independent phrases inconsequential and superfluous—is worth examining

Figure 3.1. "Rusty Pail" (structure of take one, matrix no. 37362-1)

Introduction:	4
Chorus:	
A	8
A′	8
B	8
A′	8
Blues:	
C_1	12
C_2	12
Independent phrases:	
D_1	8
D_2	8
Chorus:	
A	8
A	8
B′	8
A	8
A	8
A	8
B	8
A	8

in detail. Basically he uses two tools: first, the harmonic plan of the opening four measures of the first A phrase—a series of shifts in the underlying chords, which rock back and forth between the tonic and the subdominant—is closely paralleled to both the blues choruses (C_1, C_2) and the independent phrases (D_1, D_2). In fact, this harmonic scheme could even be said to be "developed" in its subsequent appearances, just as a motive may be developed; that is, it retains its characteristic elements and basic shape, but is altered in certain details. The original plan itself, as it unfolds in the eight measures of the A phrase in take one is rich in potential (see Figure 3.2; in this and subsequent figures, capital letters indicate major harmonies, while lowercase letters indicate minor harmonies).

Figure 3.2. (A)

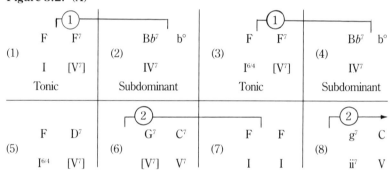

Even within the opening chorus in the repetitions of the A phrase, this scheme is not slavishly repeated; rather Waller varies one detail or another almost every time it appears. The blues chorus (C_1) reiterates the basic thrust of this plan—the shift from tonic to subdominant and back—but expands those gestures bracketed in Figure 3.2 (labeled 1 and 2) over the course of several measures (see Figure 3.3).

Figure 3.3. (C_1)

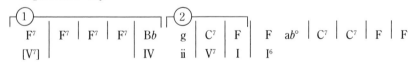

The independent phrases (D_1 and D_2) likewise preserve these gestures (see figure 3.4):

Figure 3.4. (D₁)

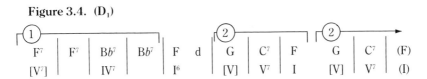

It is true that this plan relies on uncomplicated stock patterns; the gesture comprising the closing cadential pattern (labeled 2) is a cliché so firmly embedded in the style that it continues to appear in all kinds of popular music to this day. But Waller's preservation of the main thrust of the original pattern provides continuity throughout his unexpected shifts from one chorus type to the next. Furthermore, he exploits the potential of the opening gesture (1) by manipulating it in different ways—in the blues chorus by extending the first chord of the pattern (F^7) through four bars before resolving it to an unaltered major chord (Bb), and in the independent phrase by expanding to two bars each member of the original gesture (F^7 and Bb^7)—in other words, by developing it. We should note, too, that this potential for development derives in part from the lack of stability inherent in the gesture itself: the tonic chord (F) becomes a dominant seventh (F^7) resolving to another seventh of the subdominant (Bb^7), which in turn leads through a diminished chord (b°) back to the tonic. Thus, the gesture folds back on itself, and the harmonic cycle outlined lacks an unambiguous resting place; its internal dynamic quality provides a thrust that Waller capitalizes on in different ways each time it reappears in the piece.

The second device Waller uses to unify these choruses is also based on repetition of preexisting material. In this case, the repetition involves a melodic gesture that, like the harmonic gesture just discussed, is developed in appearances following its initial statement. Like the harmonic gesture, it is easily recognizable and simply constituted, consisting of a brief chromatic descent of a minor third from C to A. It initiates the blues chorus, embellished by a triplet on the opening C (Example 3.1). It also occurs in the in-

Example 3.1

dependent phrases, again at the opening, but radically altered: instead of decorating the first note, Waller extends it for four beats before outlining the motive in a new rhythmic pattern (Example 3.2). Although this motive does not appear in any similar form in the opening thirty-two-bar chorus, it nevertheless bears a relationship to the melodic content of the bridge (B phrase) of that chorus, and may well have been derived from the prominent gesture of that phrase—an interval jump outlining a minor third (Example 3.3). Indeed, the pitches emphasized in the second half of the phrase—C and A—are those of the motive as it appears in the blues and independent phrases.

Example 3.2

Example 3.3

There are still other factors that unify the diverse choruses of "Rusty Pail"—some obvious, such as the reappearance of the opening chorus material following the repeated independent phrase, and others more subtle, like the consistent use of descending melodic gestures—which further illustrate the clarity and coherence of Waller's formal design. But we should recall that, as with "I've Got a Feeling I'm Falling," the structure, although coherent, is nevertheless an element of the composition that Waller feels free to alter—that is, improvise on—in performance. Thus it is not surprising that the two extant takes of "Rusty Pail" have structures that differ in two important respects. (Indeed, since the two extant takes are the first and the third, it is possible that the structure of the third take evolved as a result of modifications Waller initiated in the second take.) In the third take (Figure 3.5) Waller lengthened what had been the first independent phrase in take one (D_1), adding four measures and thereby molding it into a blues chorus. (This phrase is referred to as "X" in Figure 3.5.) This alteration results in a hybrid phrase whose harmonic plan resembles that of the blues chorus (C), but whose melodic material retains the original motive (a descending third) of D_1 in take one, outlining it in a new, more imposing form. In the third take, then, Waller forges an even closer link between the blues chorus and the independent phrases than in the first take.

The second difference in the structure of the two takes concerns the shape of the final chorus. In take one, Waller restates the original thirty-two-bar chorus in its complete form, beginning at a *piano* dynamic level but using

Figure 3.5.   "Rusty Pail" (structure of take 3, matrix no. 37362-3)

Introduction:	4
Chorus:	
A	8
A	8
B	8
A	8
Blues:	
C_1	12
C_2	12
X	12
Independent Phrases:	
D_1	8
D_2	8
Chorus:	
A	8
A	8
B'	8
A	8
A	8
A	8
Coda:	2

a triumphant, swinging riff in the concluding phrase and ending squarely on
the last beat of the chorus's final bar. In take three, however, he begins the
final chorus *forte*, but states only the first two eight-bar phrases before shifting into a brief, two-bar coda. The reason for the difference probably lies in
Waller's insertion of the additional extended phrase (X) in take three. Of
course, playing the extra twelve bars may have left him less recording time
than he required to complete the last thirty-two-bar chorus. (Take one lasts
3'07" and take three is almost as long—2'58".) But Waller may also have had
an aesthetic reason for the insertion, involving balance and symmetry. In the
first take he concentrates his improvisational efforts on the last two thirty-
two-bar choruses. Even here, the alterations he makes, with a few significant exceptions, are rather limited in scope. In the third take, however, because the improvisation is concentrated in the central part of the piece (i.e.,
by the addition of a third twelve-bar phrase), the structure can be made symmetrical by reiterating only one complete thirty-two-bar chorus after the independent phrases, balancing the opening chorus. That is, if balance is an
aesthetic goal in "Rusty Pail," then it is achieved in both takes, but through
different formal designs. The structure of take one is defined by two roughly
equivalent members: the first consists of the opening thirty-two-bar chorus,
the two blues choruses and the two independent phrases, and the second
consists of the two final thirty-two-bar choruses. The two blues choruses
and the two independent phrases in this context represent more a development of elements exposed in the opening chorus than improvisations on
them, and the two closing thirty-two-bar choruses, which function as improvisations on the material of the opening chorus, serve to balance the first
part of the piece. In the third take, however, the design is tripartite: an
opening thirty-two-bar chorus forms the first section, the three blues
choruses (C_1, C_2, and X) and the two independent phrases comprise the
second section, and the following thirty-two-bar chorus together with the
two closing eight-bar phrases make up the third. In this scheme, Waller concentrates his improvisatory efforts in the central sections of the piece, and
thus requires only one complete thirty-two-bar chorus at the close of the
piece to balance the opening one. Again, it would be interesting to know if
the structural shape of the second take (which presumably was recorded
after the first and before the third) represented an interim stage in which
Waller partially modified the structure of the first take before reshaping it
more fully into its form in the third take.

    Waller's treatment of the harmonic plan of "Rusty Pail" is especially signif-
icant because it demonstrates that even early in his recording career he was
sensitive to the expressive possibilities of an enriched harmonic idiom. Jazz

musicians of this period tended to treat the harmonic plan of a chorus as they did its structure—that is, as a fairly fixed element throughout succeeding improvisations—and focused their creative energies on melodic and rhythmic alterations. But Waller, even as early as the mid-1920s, makes some unusual harmonic excursions that probably would not have been possible in a group situation. In take one of "Rusty Pail," for example, the harmonic plan of the bridge (B) in the opening chorus is as follows (Figure 3.6).

Figure 3.6.

d	d	B♭	E⁷	a	F⁷ E⁷	a f#°	C⁷
vi	vi	IV	[V⁷]	iii	[VI⁷] [V⁷]	iii	V⁷

What makes this progression striking and colorful is the circuitous route Waller devises to lead from the relative minor (d) back to the tonic major (F). A less interesting scheme for this maneuver might center around a single turn through the supertonic (g minor) to the dominant, resulting in the following pattern (Figure 3.7).

Figure 3.7.

d	d	A	D⁷	g	g	C⁷	C⁷
vi	vi	[V]	[V⁷]	ii	ii	V⁷	V⁷

Clearly this or any other alternative involving a straightforward progression is less compelling in and of itself than Waller's plan, and its possibilities for subsequent development are therefore much more limited. Waller's sudden shift out of the realm of d minor in the fourth bar (Figure 3.6), establishing the new tonic of a minor, and his equally sudden transition to the dominant seventh chord (C⁷) in the eighth bar increases the level of harmonic activity, thus heightening the energy of the passage.

A less creative composer might have been satisfied merely to repeat what was already an unusual scheme. Waller, however, in restating the chorus, provides this phrase (B′) with an unexpected harmonic digression (Figure 3.8).

Figure 3.8.

d	d	B♭	a	a	b° E⁷	A (e)	C⁷
vi	vi	IV	iii	iii	[ii°] [V⁷]	III	V⁷

The new pattern departs from the original, but also reinterprets it, softening the predominantly minor atmosphere by easing into A major at the close of the phrase. This alteration renders the shift from the mediant minor (a minor) back to the major tonic (F) less abrupt. Most significant, this new pattern does not occur in the third take, and we can thus be certain that it constitutes a genuine improvisation on the original harmonic scheme.

In the third take, Waller seems to place less emphasis on altering a previously outlined harmonic scheme, although this process occurs of necessity in the extension of the original eight-bar phrase (D_1) into a twelve-bar blues chorus (X). But while Waller stretches this phrase, he nevertheless manages to maintain the essence of its harmonic plan. In its original form in take one, the harmonic progression of the eight-bar phrase (D_1) appears in Figure 3.4. In take three, its elongated form in the twelve-bar phrase (X) and the modified progression of the following eight-bar phrase (D_1) are outlined in Figures 3.9 and 3.10, respectively.

Figure 3.9.

F^7 | F | F | F^7 | Bb^7 | Bb^7 b° | F C^7 | F   ab° | C^7 | C^7 | F | F
                                                      (I^6)

Figure 3.10.

F^7 | F | Bb^7 | Bb^7 | F   ab° | g C^7 | F D^7 | G   C
                              (I^6)   (I^6)

Of even greater significance than harmonic alteration in take three, however, is Waller's manipulation of the main motivic material, i.e., the brief chromatic descent through a minor third which opens phrases X, D_1, and D_2 (Examples 3.4a, 3.4b, and 3.4c respectively). By the third statement of this motive Waller has extended the descent until the gesture seems to disintegrate into a meandering solo line in the tenor range. If these three passages are compared with their counterparts from take one (Examples 3.1 and 3.2), the course of this motive's development becomes clear, from its inception as a sharply defined and rather square quarter-note descent to a sinuous, chromatic line, continuously curving downward. As a process, this development demonstrates Waller's ability to use his material both economically and elegantly. It suggests, furthermore, that during recording sessions, Waller treated subsequent takes of the same piece as opportunities for further embellishment, improvisation, and development on material originally set forth in the first take. Finally, Waller's concentration on motivic development of

Example 3.4a

Example 3.4b

Example 3.4c

this kind in the X and D phrases of take three confirms that the main thrust of his improvisational efforts occurs in the central portion of this take, not, as in take one, in the final section. Thus, for each extant take of "Rusty Pail" (and indeed, probably for each take of any piece he recorded), Waller felt free to shift the focus of his improvisational activity from one area of the piece to another.

Waller uses the special qualities of the pipe organ in his performances of "Rusty Pail" to enhance certain gestures and passages in a variety of ways. Both of the accompaniment patterns Waller devised for the organ as substitutes for the standard stride pattern of the left hand (discussed earlier in this chapter) appear. In the opening phrase of the first thirty-two-bar chorus Waller's left hand reiterates a steady series of four quarter-note pulses for each bar, supported by pedal notes on the first and third beats. He constructs a sharply contrasting figure for the melodic motive—a briskly descending gesture that he outlines in a high register with his right hand. The combination of the precise, short taps for the left-hand quarter notes with the discretely syncopated right-hand motive (whose opening pitch is placed just ahead of the beat), results in an infectious rhythmic impetus—a jaunty swing not ordinarily expected from the pipe organ. Waller's abrupt release on the organ keyboard of some of the melodic pitches, suddenly cutting off the sound, adds to the rhythmic energy of the performance.

The other accompaniment pattern Waller fashioned for the pipe organ involves quarter notes played by the left hand only on the weak (second and fourth) beats of each measure. This pattern appears primarily in situations where the prevailing dynamic level is *piano*, thus facilitating a lightening of the texture. The final thirty-two bar chorus of take one of "Rusty Pail," for example, incorporates this understated form of the accompaniment, and thus heightens the contrast to the sudden *forte* of the concluding eight-bar phrase that follows. But although the dynamic level of the concluding phrase is *forte*, Waller does not shift back to the heavier form of the accompaniment (four quarter-note chords in the left hand supported by pedal notes on the first and third beats). The closing passage incorporates a rifflike figure in the right hand—thick, four- or five-voiced chords played in a repeated rhythmic pattern—and Waller must have sensed that additional chords played in the left hand on every beat would create a texture too rich for an effective swing to develop. Waller also takes advantage of the lighter accompaniment pattern to create another new effect: because he plays the offbeat left-hand chords staccato, he can bring the notes played on the pedalboard into greater prominence by lengthening their rhythmic value from quarter notes to half notes. Treated this way, these pitches are transformed into a primitive but recognizable countermelody posed against the right-hand riff—a metamorphosis possible only on the organ.

Waller's use of differing registrations in his performances of "Rusty Pail" constitutes still another means of improvising on the original material of the piece. In both takes, for example, Waller provides a new registration (and hence, a new sound) for the bridge phrase of the thirty-two-bar chorus in its second appearance (B′ in Figures 3.1 and 3.5). In the first take, he maintains this new registration through the following eight-bar phrase (A), while in the third take he shifts back to the original registration employed for the A phrases in the first half of the chorus. Clearly then, these alternatives represent spontaneous choices, and the resulting sound produces a different effect in each instance. In the first take, Waller forges a strong continuity between the A phrases and the B phrase, while in the third take, the B phrase is isolated and emphasized by its unique color.

There is also evidence in "Rusty Pail" that Waller uses sharp registrational contrasts as an element of his compositional language. That is, he incorporates decisions concerning the choice of organ stops (and thus, the quality of sound) into the preconceived framework of the piece. Thus these choices remain fixed from one performance to the next. After the two blues phrases in both takes (C_1, C_2), for example, Waller shifts to a fuller, more grandiose sound for the subsequent phrases (D_1 in take one, X in take three). In each take, as we have seen, both sections begin with similar if not entirely identical motivic and harmonic material. This shift in registration, then, helps to differentiate the subsequent phrase in each case from the preceding blues chorus in spite of the structural ambiguity created by the similarity in material. And because the shift appears in both takes, Waller must have made the choice in advance of his performance.

In "I Ain't Got Nobody," a pipe organ solo recorded on 1 December 1927 (not quite a year after his recording of "Rusty Pail"), Waller demonstrates further his skill at integrating registration choices into the compositional process. His performance of "I Ain't Got Nobody" at this session approximates the specialized theater organ style of playing more closely than any of his

other solos of this period. At this time—1927—the theater organ still fulfilled
an important function in many American music halls, providing light music to
accompany action on stage or screen and to entertain during intermission.
Performers like John Crawford had raised the art of playing the theater organ
to a virtuoso endeavor, creating brilliant and richly varied fantasies on a variety of popular tunes. The characteristic sound of the theater organ style of
playing derived from an ornate, complex, and varied blend of timbres—a
sound facilitated by the variety of expressive possibilities and color combinations available to the performer from the organ console. In addition to a
standard set of organ stops, the theater organ included a vast array of unusual instrumental stops and sometimes outlandish special effects (whistles,
gongs, sirens, several different kinds of percussion, and so on). Furthermore, all of these different sounds could be controlled from any one of the
console's keyboards by means of couplers. Through the use of these special
characteristics, the performer could provide a distinct contrast in sound between the melodic line and the accompaniment, use a great deal of tremolo
and rapid fluctuations in dynamics, and instigate frequent shifts in registration. Any important passage or moment in the music could thus be exquisite-
ly accentuated, and each phrase of a piece would acquire its own particular
hue. These capabilities were all directed toward the objective of producing
an exaggerated, often overly melodramatic, but always immensely entertaining performance of standard popular tunes of the day. The sound may
have been ostentatious, sentimental, and teeming with surface embellishment, but for its function, it was impressively effective.

Some of these characteristics surface in the opening verse of Waller's pipe
organ performance of "I Ain't Got Nobody" (words by Roger Graham, music
by Spencer Williams).[11] The eight-bar introduction, based on the tune of the
A phrase of the chorus, is set to an unobtrusive registration: the melodic line
is played by the right hand on a four-foot flute stop, and the left hand states
the accompanying chords through the strings, flute, and vox humana stops.
The contrast between the pure, clear solo flute and the richer accompaniment combination isolates and highlights the melodic line. After this subtle
and rather pristine beginning (pristine for the theater organ, that is) Waller
fairly inundates the first line of the verse with dynamic shifts. He maintains
the opening registration, however, emphasizing the melody further by using
a light staccato touch while applying a fluid legato to the accompaniment. He
closes the verse with an exaggerated ritard, breaking the rhythmic regularity in preparation for the chorus.

In the opening line of the chorus, Waller resumes a steady pace, but re-
verses the articulation for the melody and accompaniment he had fashioned
for the verse: he outlines the melody through a smoothly connected series

of pitches while applying a light staccato to the left-hand chords. The melodic line itself ends on the first beat of the seventh measure; with almost two full measures remaining before the end of the phrase, Waller cannot resist the temptation to add a flourish of his own. Thus, while extending the final note of the line through the two concluding bars of the phrase, he concocts a melodic fragment to fill in the otherwise static break. The fragment's frivolous character, its syncopated rhythmic profile, and its prominent position above the extended final note of the melody strongly suggest that Waller's intention is to poke delicate fun at the self-pitying melancholy of the song's lyric: "I ain't got nobody, and nobody cares for me" (Example 3.5). At this point, then, Waller sheds both the accoutrements and the opulent but essentially vulgar spirit of the theater organ style.

Example 3.5

The suspicion of latent satire here is confirmed in the second statement of the chorus. As if the song were too fragile a vehicle to bear the emotional freight Waller loaded onto it in the verse and first chorus, he speeds up the tempo and applies a new registration, offering a lightly swinging interpretation of the tune in contrast to the staid progress of the previous chorus. This second chorus, essentially a jazz improvisation on the piece, also suggests that Waller's affinity for the theater organ style is limited. A performer's success in that style could be judged on his ability to create a unique sound envelope, a colorful atmosphere to surround and decorate the tune. But it was not a technique that lent itself to improvisation or to rhythmic inventiveness, and its inherent pretensions to aesthetic grandeur would have been alien to Waller's spirit. Indeed, in spite of his respect for the pipe organ, such pretensions would doubtless have attracted him as possible objects for satiric treatment.

Of course, Waller had played on theater organs during his apprenticeship at the Lincoln and Lafayette theaters, and he would do so again during his years in Cincinnati, broadcasting for his weekly radio show. But a standard American church pipe organ, which the Estey instrument in Victor's Camden studio resembled fairly closely (except for the percussion traps and the second touch capacity), differed significantly from its theater counterpart in some important respects—among them, the number of ranks of pipes, the number of ranks playable from each keyboard, the number of stops, and the special effects. Thus, Victor's Estey instrument could not really duplicate a theater organ's entire repertoire of registrations. Nor, as an instrument used for a wide variety of types of performances, many of them not popular music, was it intended to. Furthermore, Waller was not attempting a reproduction of the theater organ sound in his Camden studio recordings, although some aspects of theater organ technique do surface. Rather, the essence of Waller's solo pipe organ style had been built up from two very different foundations: an appreciation for the sacred music of the black church, which he had gained from his parents, and his extraordinary facility in stride piano technique. In these early Victor sessions, he played the pipe organ for the same aesthetic reasons he played the piano: to create jazz. In so doing, he duplicated neither stride piano nor theater organ technique, but made use of selected elements of each, thus transforming the pipe organ into an instrument of enormous rhythmic vitality and improvisational potential.

Ensemble Recordings

Waller's style in an ensemble situation differed from his approach to the pipe organ as a solo instrument in only a few particulars. Nevertheless, the combination of pipe organ and small jazz ensemble (cornet, trombone, guitar, drums), or of pipe organ with some much more unusual variety of instruments (piano, bassoon, and cornet, for example), required Waller to pay very careful attention to the problem of producing a sound that would appropriately complement the particular groups he played with. His success in matching the rhythmic energy of these groups without overpowering them amply testifies to his knowledge of the instrument and his skill at using it for jazz purposes.

With two exceptions, the group sessions were recorded in Camden with Waller playing Victor's refurbished Estey pipe organ. Significantly, these two exceptions comprise his very first recording as an organist (3 November 1926, with Fletcher Henderson and His Orchestra)[12] and a session recorded in London on 21 August 1938, long after he had stopped playing pipe organ regularly with a group. In fact, almost all Waller's pipe organ ensemble recordings were made in just three sessions in 1927 and 1928, still quite early in his recording career. The first two of these sessions produced solos, vocal accompaniments, and fourteen takes with an ensemble consisting of cornet, trombone, and drums in one session (20 May 1927), and the same instruments plus a guitar in the second session (1 December 1927). The full title accorded this group on the record label—"Thomas Waller with Morris's Hot Babies"—implied that as early as 1927 Waller had already gained a certain amount of recognition and popularity.

These recordings, then, represent Waller's first consistent efforts to integrate the pipe organ into the polyphonic texture and style of the small jazz ensemble. Each composition consisted of a series of polyphonic choruses alternating between the full ensemble and individual instrumental solos accompanied by the organ. But in spite of the often startling originality of the musicians' individual efforts,[13] the Hot Babies' recordings suffer from two features that, in a jazz performance, amount to weighty handicaps—Waller's preference for a stodgy rhythmic regularity in both full ensemble and accompaniment passages, and his use of the piano as well as the pipe organ in the same recordings. This latter instrumentation surfaces in two of the takes from the 20 May session, and in all eight takes from the 1 December session. Whether it was meant to have an arcane musical purpose or simply to confirm the possibility of a virtuosic shift from one keyboard instrument to another is not clear. But although the feat of leaping from organ to piano in a few measures' time must have required an agility surprising in a man of Waller's bulk, the evidence on the recordings suggests that it was a maneuver more appropriate to the gymnasium than to the recording studio.

Only the "Fats Waller Stomp," recorded at the 20 May session, manages to avoid the suggestion of clumsiness evident in the other takes with Morris's Hot Babies—perhaps because it is the only tune from both sessions composed solely by Waller. (One song, "Please Take Me out of Jail," is credited to both Waller and Morris; the remaining songs are by Morris or others.) Its structure, although based on alternating solo and ensemble choruses, is, as is often the case with these early Waller compositions, unique in some of its details; in other respects, it resembles, not surprisingly, a typical ragtime piece (Figure 3.11). The sequence of choruses at the opening of the piece helps accustom the listener to the organ's function as a replacement for the piano: an organ solo provides the introduction, and a series of four-bar breaks (comprising the three choruses labeled A in Figure 3.11) serves to contrast the sound of a solo instrument accompanied by the organ with that of the full ensemble in which the organ plays a more subsidiary role. Thus the organ's solo breaks in the A_3 chorus have been well prepared. This same instrumental sequence—two choruses played by solo instruments accompanied by organ—has been built into three consecutive choruses later in the piece, for example, the C choruses. In addition, the structural plan involves a recapitulation of previously stated material, including the introductory organ solo, at the close of the piece. Here, however,

Figure 3.11. **"Fats Waller Stomp" (structure of take 2, matrix no. 38050-2)**

Introduction:	4	(organ)
A_1	16	(trumpet + organ—4, ensemble—4, trumpet + organ—4, ensemble—4)
A_2	16	(trombone + organ—4, ensemble—4, trombone + organ—4, ensemble—4)
A_3	16	(solo organ—4, ensemble—4, solo organ—4, ensemble—4)
B_1	16	(8 + 8)—ensemble
B_2	16	(8 + 8)—ensemble
C_1	16	(8 + 8)—trumpet
C_2	16	(8 + 8)—trombone
C_3	16	(8 + 8)—organ
B_3	16	(8 + 8)—ensemble
A_4	16	(trumpet + organ—4, ensemble—4, trumpet + organ—4, ensemble—4)
Coda:	4	(organ, based on Introduction)
	4	(ensemble, new material)

the order in which the material appears has been reversed, and the length of the phrases truncated. Nonetheless, this mirror-image recapitulation reveals Waller's sophisticated approach to the complexities of structure, especially in terms of his preference for balanced forms. This characteristic alone would suffice to distinguish the "Fats Waller Stomp" from the other Morris's Hot Babies recordings. But rhythmically, too, it is more compelling than its companion pieces of the session. When the B_1 chorus is restated (B_3), for example, Waller fashions the straightforward pattern first heard in the series of chromatically descending chords in B_1 into a strongly syncopated pattern (Figure 3.12).

Figure 3.12.

Elsewhere in the piece, Waller makes use of syncopations that relieve the predictability of his usual accompaniment pattern. The stop-time accompaniment behind the solo breaks of the A choruses involves the repetition of a dominant seventh chord in the following configuration (Figure 3.13).

Figure 3.13.

Thus, we can speculate that had Waller recorded a greater number of his own compositions with Morris's Hot Babies, the group might have played a more adventurous and compelling kind of jazz. But we can also assert, based on the evidence of the Louisiana Sugar Babes session on 27 March 1928, that the abilities of the instrumentalists Waller played with had as profound an effect on the eventual success of the performance as the quality of the musical material. For the 27 March session, the Victor producer Ralph Peer assembled an extraordinary group: Waller on the pipe organ, Jabbo Smith on cornet, Garvin Bushell on clarinet, alto sax, and, oddly enough, bassoon, and Waller's friend and mentor, James P. Johnson, on the piano.[14] Peer had apparently heard Waller and Johnson playing duets during the intermission of the musical show "Keep Shufflin'," for which both men had composed music. The producer decided to record the two pianists together, and recruited Smith and Bushell from the show's pit band for the session as well. The novel instrumentation, coupling piano and pipe organ, eliminating percussion, and using bassoon as an occasional (and for jazz, unheard-of) substitute for the clarinet or sax, produced a unique sound.[15] Often what would have been, in a conventional group situation, a chorus for solo instrument accompanied by keyboard and other rhythmic instruments, was transformed into a joint enterprise between the soloist and the keyboard player. The lead instrument still retained an edge of prominence over its accompaniment, but through the inventiveness and skill of Waller and Johnson, their role in the performance was elevated from accompanist to partner. Of course, in the choruses designated for piano and organ, this approach meant that their contributions were of equal importance; they were, in fact, playing improvised duets, as they had been doing on two pianos during the intermissions of "Keep Shufflin'."

Peer's foresight resulted in a series of recordings in which the organ is a fully integrated member of the ensemble. Several passages from the first take of "Willow Tree" (matrix no. 42566-1), a Waller composition, reveal the intricacy and strength of the organ's relationship to the solo instruments and to the piano. The structure of the piece is simple: a four-bar introduction precedes three statements of a thirty-two-bar AABA chorus; two four-bar verse phrases separate the first and second statements of the chorus. In the first phrase of the opening chorus, the piano is more prominent than the organ, although both instruments make use of the same basic material. Johnson and Waller mold the melody to take advantage of the sound characteristics of their respective instruments. Johnson's highly decorated line and the improvised chordal fragment he adds at the close of the phrase provide an ornamental veneer to the simpler melodic shape Waller outlines (Example 3.6). Johnson's barrage of ornamentation on the piano helps foster the illusion of a continuous stream of melody, thereby overcoming the inherent handicap facing the pianist who has to compete simultaneously against an organ: the piano's sound decays quickly, while the organ's sonority can be more evenly sustained.

Example 3.6

The second statement of the chorus provides strong corroboration of Waller's sensitivity to his role in this session as a partner rather than an accompanist. Here, the alto saxophone presents the melody, undecorated, much as the organ had done in the first statement of the chorus. But unlike the organ, which had to remain in the background in order not to overwhelm the piano, the sax plays its melodic line prominently in the foreground. Waller simply adopts the piano's former function: he provides an embroidered line as a countermelody, but plays it in a subdued registration, complementing the sax without covering it (Example 3.7). This new function for the organ

Example 3.7

becomes most explicit in the last two bars of the phrase, where the sax extends the closing pitch of the line (as the organ had done behind the piano in the first chorus—Example 3.6), while the organ plays a florid embellished line above it.

In "Persian Rug," the final tune recorded by the Louisiana Sugar Babes, the organ adopts a somewhat different yet parallel role. An eight-bar piano introduction and a sixteen-bar segment for organ precede the main material of the piece—four thirty-two-bar AABA choruses. The solo organ states the first thirty-two-bar chorus; the next chorus is played by muted trumpet with piano accompaniment. In his solo chorus, Waller outlines the melody in a relatively straightforward manner, using a registration with a pure, hollow timbre. This registration contrasts sharply with that of the preceding six-teen-bar segment, in which the oboe and cornopean stops together create a focused, reedy sound. But Waller's choice of the new registration has a pur-pose more significant than simply to provide contrast: the timbre of the solo organ chorus closely resembles that of the muted trumpet solo in the follow-ing chorus. By thus linking the timbre of the solo melodic lines in the two consecutive choruses, Waller renders the shift from organ to piano accom-paniment less jarring. Here, then, Waller demonstrates both his talent at integrating the organ into the texture of a small jazz ensemble, and his skill in still another important aspect of ensemble playing—the transition from one instrumental timbre to another. In this passage, as indeed in all the Lou-isiana Sugar Babes sides, the judicious use of the pipe organ's special capa-bilities helps Waller to overcome its seemingly severe liabilities as a jazz instrument.

James P. Johnson played an equally important role in the level of musical excellence achieved by the Louisiana Sugar Babes. In "Willow Tree," John-son's piano constantly shifts ground, moving between melodic prominence and background chordal and rhythmic support for the other instruments. When the organ outlines foreground melodic material (mm. 37–44) the piano maintains rhythmic energy behind it with a series of chords played on each beat. This marchlike regularity provides a sharp edge to the organ's legato phrasing, tightening the rhythmic control. But Johnson carefully includes a sophisticated musical commentary on the melodic material as well: Waller outlines a motive in the soprano range of the organ, which Johnson echoes, mid-phrase, in the piano's baritone register (Example 3.8).

Example 3.8

The final chorus of both "Willow Tree" takes begins with two eight-bar phrases of piano-organ duet, a situation duplicated in "Persian Rug" and in the two takes of "Thou Swell." These passages demonstrate the different but extraordinarily compatible styles of Waller and Johnson on their respective instruments. Johnson's piano improvisations on the material are pure stride—a swinging left-hand pattern, parallel fourths and other "tricks" in the right hand, repeated melodic embellishments—while Waller uses both an electric staccato touch and long, sustained tones to maximize the organ's range of expressive possibilities. Yet the degree of interdependence between these simultaneously improvised solos bespeaks an intuitive response in both performers to each other's music, style, and approach. Especially in take one of "Thou Swell" (matrix no. 42568-1; mm. 129–44), Waller and Johnson anticipate and complement each other's gestures, interweaving the organ and piano parts on such a detailed level in this passage that the musical result projects the balance and control of a carefully worked out composition. The melodic lines intertwine like strands of an especially profuse vine; the embellishments, although lush, neither sap the rhythmic energy nor weigh the phrase down with extraneous material. Yet there can be no doubt that both performers were improvising: the parallel passage in the second take of "Thou Swell" is substantially different. To improvise a coherent solo is difficult enough; to improvise keyboard duets that are coherent, exciting, and musically satisfying represents a significant—indeed, an astonishing— achievement not often duplicated in the annals of early jazz.

Vocal Accompaniments

Waller recorded a total of only nine songs as an accompanist on the pipe organ for different singers (seven for Victor and two for HMV in London).[16]

Of this small total we may discount the four titles recorded at the Camden studios on 14 November 1927. These four, plus a pipe organ solo recorded at the same session, were made as a gesture to the memory of the black actress and singer Florence Mills, whose premature death on 1 November 1927 had profoundly affected all of Harlem. Various accounts of her life alluded to her extraordinary popularity in the black community; that five separate songs were recorded in her honor by Victor alone testifies to the esteem in which she was held by all elements of Harlem society. But the recordings also show that Victor producers understood the so-called "race" market well enough to realize that the appearance of Florence Mills's name in a song's title would probably ensure its commercial success as a record. Issuing these discs thus represented an astute and lucrative marketing move, if also a cynical and calculated one. A more subtle measure of Mills's stature can be deduced from Waller's understated accompaniments for two of the vocalists in the two takes from this session that survive. Although these songs are of an excessively sentimental and religious nature, and although they are sung in an exaggerated manner, Waller's playing contains not a hint of satire. Of course, Waller only first began to exploit his gift for comedy on recordings in vocal performances made for Columbia in 1931, some four years later. Still, we know that he had been cultivating his gifts as an entertainer much earlier in his career, as organist at the Lincoln and Lafayette theaters, and it is therefore difficult to believe that sentimentality of this magnitude would have passed without some cheeky comment from him unless he were entirely sincere in expressing it.

Three of the five remaining recordings teamed Waller on pipe organ with blues singer Alberta Hunter at the same 20 May 1927 session during which Waller recorded with Morris's Hot Babies. He also recorded pipe organ solos of each of the three songs sung by Hunter at this session; comparisons between the vocal and solo versions afford us the opportunity of establishing what particular modifications in his style Waller made when accompanying. Waller had already accompanied Hunter on piano in 1923, and in fact had recorded with several other noted blues singers in the 1920s as well (among them Sara Martin in 1922 and 1923, Hazel Meyers in 1924, Caroline Johnson in 1926, and Maude Mills in 1927). At this stage, then, he was already an experienced accompanist in the blues idiom and had worked successfully with Hunter herself on a previous occasion.

As in other situations in which multiple takes of the same piece were made, Waller varies the structure of the piece from one version to the next.[17] A comparison of the structures of the two versions of "Beale Street Blues" demonstrates that Waller felt a greater degree of freedom to improvise throughout the solo version than in any passage in the vocal version. In the first and second blues choruses of the vocal version, for example (Figure 3.14a), Waller adheres closely to the melodic line, distinguishing the second chorus from the first only through the simplest of variation devices—raising the line an octave. Although he does create a syncopated solo bass line on the organ's pedals in the fourth chorus, the other solo passages for organ lack any real daring or originality. In the pipe organ version (Figure 3.14b), however, Waller incorporates a much greater variety of melodic and harmonic invention. (This is partly a consequence of the appreciably faster tempo of the pipe organ version, which enables Waller to increase the length of this take beyond that of the vocal version by two twelve-bar blues choruses plus an extra eight-bar verse phrase. It is probable, given the order of the matrix numbers of the two versions, that the vocal version, no. 38046, was recorded prior to the pipe organ version, no. 38047. By speeding up the tempo, therefore, Waller could have planned for the additional choruses, anticipating that the greater number of choruses would accommodate a greater amount and variety of improvisation than had been possible in the vocal version.)

Oddly enough, in contrast to the two "Beale Street Blues" performances, it is the vocal version of "Sugar," not the solo pipe organ take, into which Waller incorporates his more adventurous improvisations. During the sung choruses, Waller's right hand tends mainly to double Hunter's melodic line,

Figure 3.14a. "Beale St. Blues" (structure of Alberta Hunter vocal, matrix no. 38046-2)

Introduction:	4
Blues Choruses:	
1	12
2	12
Verse:	
X	8
Blues Choruses:	
3	12
4	12
5 (vocal)	12
6 (vocal)	12

**Figure 3.14b. "Beale St. Blues" (structure of Pipe Organ solo, matrix
no. 38047-1)**

Introduction:	4
Blues Choruses:	
1	12
2	12

Verse:	
X	8
X'	8

Blues Choruses:	
3	12
4	12
5	12
6	12
7	12
8	12

as it does when he accompanies himself in the performances of spirituals
recorded with electric organ. (This represents, of course, a significant de-
parture from his approach to accompanying an instrument, where, as we
saw in the Louisiana Sugar Babes session, he devised a line that in some way
contrasted with that of the solo instrument rather than simply doubled it. But
the reason for this different approach may lie in the fact that counterpoint,
which results from two simultaneous but contrasting melodic lines, constitutes an essential component of early instrumental jazz, while in a performance involving a text, comprehension of the words is a paramount
consideration.) Perhaps to compensate for this modesty in his role as accompanist, Waller creates a solo in the one thirty-two-bar chorus for solo pipe
organ that is much more elaborate than any passage of the pipe organ version. It is as if all of his improvisatory ideas, which in the pipe organ version
could be spread over the space of three choruses, here must be telescoped
into just one brief thirty-two-bar chorus. Hunter must in some way have
sensed the extent of Waller's efforts, for she registers her approval during
the bridge of his solo by enthusiastically commenting, "Plonk that thing,
Fats!"

There are other significant differences between the two versions of "Sugar" as well. The key of the instrumental version (matrix no. 38044-1) is F

major, but that of the vocal version (matrix no. 38045-2) is E*b* major. Waller had to transpose the song down a whole step in order to accommodate the singer. As we have already seen in chapter 2, transposition requires a knowledge of music theory; thus these two versions provide tangible evidence of Waller's experience as an accompanist and the degree of his technical expertise. Furthermore, only in the vocal version of "Sugar" (in contrast to both "Beale Street Blues" and "I'm Goin' to See My Ma") does Hunter maintain a substantial presence; two of the three thirty-two-bar choruses in the piece are sung, as is the sixteen-bar verse section. In "Beale Street Blues," only the last two of a total of six blues choruses are sung, and in "I'm Goin' to See My Ma," Hunter sings only the sixteen-bar verse and one thirty-two-bar chorus.

The other two recordings on which Waller plays pipe organ to accompany a singer were made in London on 28 August 1938 at the Abbey Road studios of His Master's Voice. The singer was Adelaide Hall, who had appeared in a number of musicals and nightclub revues in Harlem in the 1920s and early 1930s; the instrument Waller played was a Compton theater organ. Waller had by this time developed a highly individual style as a jazz musician, and this performance is thus distinguished from the earlier organ accompaniments by his use of the improvised melodic gestures, chromatic flourishes, and polished (but modified) stride figures, which he had absorbed into his musical vocabulary. But like any good jazz musician, Waller was sensitive to the musical ambience of his surroundings—that is, to the quality of the instrument he was playing and to the abilities of the musicians he was working with. In this instance, the exaggerated effects possible on the instrument—massive tremolo, heavy accents generated by second touch capability, and the abundance of unusual timbres—combined with the operatic and slightly cloying quality of Hall's voice to create performances that, in spite of some mild improvisation, belong more to the music-hall tradition than to jazz. Waller could, however, redeem even the most unpromising situations. In this instance, as so often with his own renditions of mediocre lyrics, Waller interpolates comments, humorous asides, and questions with which he reinterprets the lyrics. He also engages in a dialogue with the singer, teasing her and destroying any semblance of a straight performance. To her credit, Hall demonstrates an independence of her own in this performance, and catches the spirit of Waller's humor; on the second title recorded, "I Can't Give You Anything But Love, Baby," she emends the opening line of the text for the second chorus by singing, "I can't give you anything but love, my little fat baby," to which Waller petulantly replies, "Oh baby, don't talk like that."

At this same London session, Waller recorded four spirituals ("Swing

Low, Sweet Chariot," "All God's Chillun Got Wings," "Go Down, Moses," and "Deep River") and two other songs from the black folk repertoire ("Water Boy" and "Lonesome Road") as pipe organ solos on the Compton organ. His performances of the spirituals radiate an intensity totally absent from the accompaniments for Adelaide Hall. In part, of course, he is responsible only to himself for the musical result; he does not need to take another performer's style into consideration. In part, however, the nature of the musical material is also a crucial factor. Although he did not often record or perform sacred music (a category that, for Waller, would include spirituals), it nevertheless retained its special power for him throughout his career. We can deduce the importance he attached to spirituals by the fact that at this session, he recorded two separate vocal versions *and* one instrumental version of each title.[18] The vocal versions of all four spirituals were rejected by HMV, but Waller recorded three of them again in 1939 for Victor, accompanying himself this time on electric organ.

A comparison between these two sets of performances (1938 and 1939) reveals a fundamental difference in approach. The Compton organ, with its multitude of timbral possibilities and special effects, was well suited to the kind of interpretation Waller evidently wanted at the 1938 session—a series of rhapsodic, freely constructed variations in which he imposes almost every imaginable style, from bombastic to refined, on these simple tunes. Yet in spite of the exaggerated and sudden changes from one verse to the next—a suggestion, in fact, of the theater organ style—the whole seems to make a unified performance; perhaps it is simply that Waller could expect his listeners to be completely familiar with the melodic material of the spirituals, and no excesses in performance could destroy the underlying cohesion of the piece. "Swing Low, Sweet Chariot," for example, consists of a lengthy and flamboyant introduction, a chorus, and a statement of the verse followed by two more choruses. The first chorus is performed almost arhythmically: Waller isolates the phrases, pausing for irregular periods of silence between each one. This kind of phrasing probably derives from that most traditional and venerable of black musical institutions, congregational singing. Waller assigns the preacher's role to the organ, treating each line individually, starting and stopping unpredictably, and emphasizing moments of emotional intensity through special effects, accents, or sudden pauses. (The most convincing and dramatic example of this effect, however, occurs not in the spirituals, but in "Water Boy," where Waller plays the opening line unaccompanied, in a halting, improvisatory style that reflects the passionate plea of the text.) Like any good blues musician, then, Waller makes his instrument substitute successfully for his voice—that is, he makes it "sing"—by striving to duplicate on the organ what his voice might do with the tune. The difference in approach on the 1939 vocal version of "Swing Low, Sweet Chariot," therefore, comes as even more of a surprise; Waller sings the song in a completely straightforward manner, without embellishing the tune vocally or indulging in any rhythmic freedom. The organ accompaniment is almost excessively prim, providing a subtle beat behind the merest outline of a harmonic foundation. There is nevertheless a sense of conviction in this uncomplicated rendition, communicated by the intensity in Waller's voice (for example, when he reaches for a high G on the phrase "band of angels"). And the performance is not devoid of subtle variation, either; Waller lends a limpid delicacy to the shading of the words "sweet chariot" in the first chorus, while in the second chorus he contrasts these words with the surrounding text by suddenly speaking them, in a syncopated rhythmic pattern, using a throaty stage whisper. Following the vocal portion of the song, Waller adds three choruses for organ solo. He improvises on the tune to some extent in this portion of the performance, but the melodic embellishments seem conservative when compared to the 1938 London session, and the performance acquires a staid and uneventful quality from this point on. Even the sudden increase in tempo for the last chorus fails to energize the solo. Nevertheless, the vocal portion of this 1939 version of "Swing Low, Sweet Chariot," at least, stands as an interesting alternative to the 1938 pipe organ version. In spite of the stylistic differences between them, both offer interpretations of a traditional song from the sacred repertoire of black folk music that reflect not only Waller's sensitivity to a text, but also the depth of his religious convictions.

Waller imbues all six of the pipe organ solos recorded at the 1938 London session—the four spirituals and the two folk songs—with the improvisational, sometimes passionate atmosphere of his "Swing Low" performance at that session, and this sets them all apart from his performances of commercial songs. His aim is less to entertain, it seems, than to commune. He remains sensitive to the text of each individual song, varying the musical atmosphere in accordance with the emotional quality of the text. The essentially positive message of "All God's Chillun Got Wings"—a statement of hope and affirmation—is reflected in Waller's light, staccato touch, choppy (but regular) phrasing, fanciful registrations, and capricious, almost humorous ending. "Deep River," like "Swing Low," is more meditative. "Go Down, Moses" is perhaps the most intense—rhapsodic and rhythmically free in the first chorus, as if spontaneously preached, but driving and fiercely energetic

in the final one. Waller seems to be interpreting the lyrics first in an imploring
and then in a demanding tone. In the central verse, he relaxes this intensity
by concentrating on a purely musical means of variation, as opposed to a
dramatic one. He surrounds the melodic line with a sinuous chromatic countermelody, constantly ascending and descending the scale (Example 3.9).
The introduction of polyphonic texture—a relatively sophisticated musical
device—into an otherwise powerful and direct interpretation provides some
momentary relief from the passion of the other verses.

Example 3.9

   This combination of technical skill and emotional intensity informs all the
performances of the spirituals; in retrospect, then, it is appropriate that the
spirituals should have been the final solo pipe organ performances of Waller's
career. Although not strictly jazz performances, they rely for their immediacy and power on a combination of essentially jazz techniques and a consistently judicious exploitation of the organ's special timbral capabilities. As in
his earlier pipe organ solos, Waller employs original and carefully conceived
combinations of stops to separate the melodic line from the accompaniment,
and registrational shifts to distinguish one phrase (or chorus) from subsequent ones. As he does in his performances with small ensembles, he incorporates accompaniment patterns for the pedals and the left hand, which,

while not duplicating the left-hand patterns characteristic of stride piano, serve essentially the same harmonic and rhythmic functions. But as always, the melody remains the preeminent strand of the musical fabric for Waller. He enhances it with discrete or florid embellishments, as his aesthetic purpose dictates, and he imbues it with emotional power by controlling phrasing and accentuation.

Finally, the performances of the spirituals closely resemble Waller's best jazz performances in the quality of his improvisations—the delicate melodic figures, the flexible phrasing, the structural and harmonic freedom, and the rhythmic propulsion and energy of his swing balanced by an often unpredictable rhythmic freedom. Waller was in many ways at the height of his powers as a jazz pianist and improviser in 1938; the 1938 recordings of the spirituals demonstrate conclusively that he could draw freely and fully on those powers when playing the pipe organ. Even though by this time he had not performed regularly on the pipe organ for many years, he still played it with a profound and intuitive understanding of its nature. It remained his favorite instrument, one on which he could and did create moving and exciting jazz.

4

Transformations

In 1932 Waller began broadcasting regularly for station WLW in Cincinnati, Ohio. He continued his activity at the station for almost two years, but apparently made no recordings during that time.[1] Thereafter, he returned to New York and signed an exclusive recording contract with Victor, an agreement that turned out to have unforeseen consequences for him. For the first time in his career, Waller gained a steady income and regular recording dates. And for its part, by adding an already well-established musician and entertainer to its roster, Victor was assured of continued profits from its investment. But the company's producers no longer sought to record Waller as a jazz pianist, as they had in the late 1920s; instead, in order to capitalize on Waller's success as a popular entertainer, they chose a repertoire for him to record that consisted almost entirely of commercial Tin Pan Alley ditties. Thus the pianist's business relationship with the company resulted in an important change in the music he played and recorded at this juncture in his career.

Waller's liaison with Victor may also have had an impact on the actual recording routine he followed in the studio, although this is more difficult to document. Still, we cannot fail to notice the intriguing fact that the use of multiple takes as a routine procedure was restricted to the sessions before 1930; after 1934, when Waller formalized his association with Victor through the exclusive contract, multiple takes were made only infrequently. There are several possible reasons for this change in routine. First, the company may not have been able to afford either the time or materials for extra takes—these were, after all, the years of the Great Depression. Second, as we have already noted, many of the songs recorded by Waller after 1934 could be classified as second-rate; the pianist and his band may have felt that they could produce at least an adequate performance in one take, thereby sparing themselves the necessity for subsequent rehearsing and polishing of basically uninteresting material. Third, both Waller and his band were by this time so accomplished that after running through a number or rehearsing it, the first take could have represented their best performance anyway. In my view, however, the most likely reason is that Victor may simply have had less stake in the inherent musical quality of the performances than previously, in the late 1920s, when Waller recorded for the company primarily as a stride pianist. And since the terms of the contract would not permit Waller to record for any other company, Victor's executives would not need to be concerned with Waller's own degree of satisfaction with the finished recording; as long as its commercial potential was sufficient, the company's criterion for a successful take was fulfilled.

As I suggested in chapter 2 with respect to Waller's singing, some white jazz critics and historians have assumed that by the time he began his association with Victor, Waller had already drifted away from jazz and into the world of popular entertainment. They tend to focus on three aspects of Waller's work during these years: the commercial nature of the musical material he was given to work with at Victor, the lack of accommodation in the recording routine to the exigencies of genuine improvisation, and the superficial similarities among the performances themselves (the standard approach to form; the satirization of the lyrics, often involving the same or related humorous asides; and similar musical gestures). For these critics, such factors appear to obscure Waller's real achievements in the Victor recordings. Max Harrison, for example, writing in *Jazz on Record*, laments what he considers the loss to jazz of Waller's gifts in this period. In an odd but revealing balancing act of criticism, Harrison shifts from praising the pianist's potential to belittling much of his playing:

Waller's is probably the saddest case of misspent talent which jazz on records can show. His output suggests he had all the gifts a jazzman needs except the tough, almost ruthless temperament usually necessary for the truest creative achievements. . . . Part of his trouble was that the rigid, all-too successful framework led Waller to fall back on pretty decoration rather than to dig deep and produce his best. But whenever he escapes that formula the result is strikingly fresh and thoughtful music. Alas, this did not happen often enough for his talents to grow as they might have done. [2]

Harrison takes no pains to disguise his ambivalence: he recognizes Waller's abilities, but because he cannot reconcile those abilities with his low estimate of most of Waller's output he vacillates between admiration and skepticism.

His assessment presents other difficulties as well. Harrison stipulates criteria for excellence that are essentially irrelevant to an appraisal of jazz, or,
for that matter, of any kind of music: ". . . he had all the gifts a jazzman
needs except the tough, almost ruthless temperament usually necessary for
the truest creative achievements." Generalizations that equate a particular
type of personality—in this case, "almost ruthless"—with the ability to produce "the truest achievements" in art are always a little risky: by this criterion, how are we to account for the accomplishments of quieter, gentler
musicians—Franz Schubert, say, or Lester Young? Then, too, Harrison
seems to imply that Waller was facile, perhaps even lazy—that he did not
use his talent as assiduously and productively as he should have. "Part of his
trouble was that the rigid, all-too successful framework led Waller to fall back
on pretty decoration rather than to dig deep and produce his best." Two
problems emerge from this characterization of Waller's compositional approach. First, by suggesting that Waller chose to "fall back on" decoration,
Harrison accuses the pianist of a double failure: failure to *work* at generating
ideas, and failure to actually *produce* ideas of genuine substance. But the
amount of time and effort a musician invests in the process of improvisation
is not really germane to the quality of his conceptions themselves, and in any
case, far from "falling back" on anything, Waller embellishes his melodies
with particular care and skill and originality. Second, by characterizing Waller's decoration as "pretty," Harrison casts Waller's use of stride figures
(which is, in a sense, a process of ornamentation) in a pejorative light, as if
the process itself were a superficial, even trivial one, somehow not aesthetically profound enough to qualify as among the "truest creative achievements." Possibly this hierarchy derives from critical dogma commonly held
for Western European music; yet jazz, an art form created by black Americans, has entirely different criteria for aesthetic profundity than those Harrison specifies. Further, Harrison's indictment of Waller's supposed use of a
"formula" misses the point because he fails to recognize when and how the
formula is used. Every great jazz performer has a repertoire of musical gestures that appear and reappear in a variety of contexts. But such gestures
are always manipulated and altered in myriad ways, and it is the jazz critic's
task in part to establish what those changes are and what they signify. (As
we have already seen, stride piano is a language whose rhetoric depends on
just such formulas as those Harrison disparages.) Finally, Harrison's assertion that Waller failed to "dig deep and produce his best" represents, to my
mind, a simple prejudice. What does it mean to "dig deep"? Can Harrison be
certain that Waller didn't? Is digging deep—whatever it may be—essential

to great jazz, or is this yet another judgment carried over from a set of assumptions and values related to music of Western European origin?

I suspect a kind of elitism may be at work here: once a performing artist achieves commercial success, the charge of having "sold out"—of having abandoned truly creative work in exchange for producing competent but predictable performances that will guarantee economic security—will inevitably be leveled at the artist. The subtext of this argument is that only those artists who have not achieved popularity (i.e., who are "misunderstood" by the public) can produce anything aesthetically worthwhile. Harrison's stance also implies that Waller's easygoing style and witty delivery may somehow have diminished the value of his performances. But again, such an attitude would deny the possibility that for black performers, humorous delivery and serious aesthetic goals can coexist without contradiction. No less an authority than Dizzy Gillespie has indicated that humor—and specifically, Fats Waller's kind of humor—can be a crucial component of jazz performance. In response to the criticism that he (Gillespie) indulged in too much antic behavior while performing—that he should, in effect, be more "serious" about his music— Gillespie stated "I am serious about music, but I like to have fun, too. Fats Waller always had fun, and he was my main man."[3]

Ultimately, then, the contradictory aspects of appraisals like Harrison's arise in my view not from Waller's music but from the critics' own conflicting responses to a successful, funny, popular black entertainer who also happened to be a superb and profoundly influential jazz musician. Harrison's assessment thus exemplifies the major pitfall much writing on Waller's later recordings tumbles into: failure to analyze in detail the actual content of Waller's improvisations. Such analysis demonstrates that the effects of Waller's business liason with Victor, although clear in terms of the commercial nature of the repertoire imposed on the pianist, were neither so profound nor detrimental as might be assumed. And even though some of the recorded evidence for this assertion may not have been available to Harrison and others, since it occasionally surfaces in unissued takes which have only recently (i.e., since 1972) been released for the first time, there are many well-known performances that demonstrate the consistently rich and rewarding quality of Waller's gifts (see note 10). One cannot dispute that Waller and his usual group ("Fats Waller and His Rhythm") recorded a substantial amount of material that, in its original form, could be described as hackwork popular songs. As prospective jazz pieces, these ditties were seemingly hopeless. Yet with the often able assistance of his group, Waller managed to lift even the most banal and overworked musical clichés into the realm of jazz.

"I Got Rhythm"

On 29 November 1935, "Fats Waller and His Rhythm" recorded six titles for
Victor. These sides, although they lack any real flashes of energy or sophisticated ideas in improvisation, at least serve to demonstrate the group's
competence as a jazz ensemble, and all six were issued by Victor. Five days
later, on 4 December 1935, the group returned to the Victor studio, supplemented on this occasion by five additional musicians—thereby almost doubling its normal complement of six. (One of the extra musicians was pianist
Hank Duncan, a student and protégé of Waller's. The reason for this unusual
instrumentation—the inclusion of two pianists in one jazz ensemble, even
one of this size, was a rare, if not unique, phenomenon—will shortly become
clear.) The group recorded three titles—two takes of "Fat and Greasy" (matrix nos. 98196-1 and -2), and one each of "Functionizin'" (matrix no. 98197-
1) and "I Got Rhythm" (matrix no. 98198-1). But while Victor's producers
had approved all the takes from the 29 November session for issue, none of
those from the 4 December session was ever released. To be sure, both
"Fat and Greasy" and "Functionizin'" are not notably energetic performances, and the earthy lyrics to "Fat and Greasy" could have been taken by
Victor's executives as even more objectionable when sung by Waller than
they were on the page. But the third title from the later session, "I Got
Rhythm" (words by Ira Gershwin, music by George Gershwin), although a
standard in the repertoire and a brilliant jazz interpretation in this version,
may well have been considered the most provocative and least acceptable
performance of the three. Indeed, the very circumstances that render it
unique probably contributed to Victor's verdict not to issue it.

   The arranger Don Donaldson had fashioned a fairly typical big band arrangement of the Gershwin tune for the band; nevertheless, a loose, improvisatory atmosphere prevails, fostered by a great deal of verbal banter
thrown back and forth between Waller and the members of the ensemble.
To some degree, this atmosphere must have been planned, and the banter
rehearsed. Maurice Waller, in his biography of his father, reports that a
group similar to the one that recorded on 4 December toured the northeast
earlier in the same year (1935), including performances of "I Got Rhythm" in
its repertoire. Although some confusion concerning the personnel for the
tour arises from Maurice's report,[4] it is at least possible that many of the
same musicians who participated in the tour are also present on the 4 December recording. And Maurice's description of the group's performance of
"I Got Rhythm" on tour is fairly consistent with the basic thrust and structure
of the recorded version.

The tempo of the 4 December performance is extremely fast—so fast that Waller at one point slurs and growls his way through the lyrics. His rendition is not careless, however, although the producers might have perceived it that way; Waller simply chooses to improvise from the start, altering both text and music without first stating the tune in its original shape. (This song was so well known by the end of 1935—it was written and composed in 1930 and introduced in that same year by Ethel Merman in the Broadway musical "Girl Crazy"—that Waller could justifiably assume his audience would have heard it before. Furthermore, in Donaldson's arrangement, the saxes had already stated the tune in the opening instrumental chorus.) In his singing, Waller pulls the rhythmic configurations of each two-measure group all out of shape, consistently lingering behind the beat. Then, in the last eight-measure phrase of the chorus, he catches up with himself and puts each syllable of the words "I got rhythm" squarely on each strong beat. The trombone (Benny Morton) takes a solo on the next chorus, except for the bridge, which is taken by the tenor sax. During the first part of Morton's solo, Waller encourages him every two measures or so with carefully syncopated commentary: "Swing it on out [there, yes] . . . yes, yes . . . my, my . . . well, all right! Uh, huh . . . yes, yes." This is followed by a fast-moving solo from Rudy Powell on clarinet which includes a quotation of the opening of "Yankee Doodle."

The next chorus—the fifth—is Hank Duncan's solo on piano, and it is at this point that this version of "I Got Rhythm" becomes a historical document of some significance. For the dialogue between Waller and the members of the band that ensues during Duncan's solo makes clear that a friendly but serious competition is taking place between Duncan and Waller. Given the spirit of competitiveness that flourished among the first generation of stride pianists, what we witness in these two solo choruses is nothing less than a miniature old-fashioned cutting contest, fueled by Waller's boisterous challenges and mock-injured pride. This re-creation of the performance ambience of a by this time anachronistic style first took place, if Maurice's account is to be believed, on the tour of early 1935. It is equally clear from his description, however, that the version of "I Got Rhythm" performed by the group on tour differed in many details from the recorded one.

Dad and the other pianist, Hank Duncan, had a bit of funny business which brought the house down everywhere. It was a piano duel reminiscent of Dad's contests with James P. in *Keep Shufflin'*. Hank would burst into a rousing chorus of "I Got Rhythm." . . . From across the stage would flash a patented Waller look, eyebrows raised in feigned disbelief. Duncan then topped the first chorus with some dazzling musicianship. Dad would turn to the audience and comment, "Say, this guy can really play!" Then he would take over, besting Duncan, and the duel was on. The two of them would end the song with a fantastic duel that socked the audience.[5]

Thus, although the song's arrangement remained intact for the recording, the dialogue and the solos surely differed. The recording's improvisatory atmosphere may have been premeditated, but the actual content of the solos was not, and they qualify, therefore, as genuine improvisations.

There is an interesting social dynamic at work in the group during the piano solos; as spectators, it is inevitable that members of the band should express partisanship towards one or the other of the two contestants. From what we can decipher of the musicians' commentary in the background, it is Duncan, not Waller, who enlists the group's support and sympathy. Perhaps because Duncan, although ten years Waller's senior, is Waller's protégé, he is perceived as the underdog. By siding with him the band may see itself as evening up the odds. But there is another effect derived from the banter and the partisanship. Waller's challenges (if they were any less friendly, they would be taunts) are designed to provoke Duncan into trying maneuvers that are increasingly brilliant and technically more difficult; the band, by championing Duncan, intends to spur Waller on to the same goal. The more this competitive element is stressed by everyone, the more likely it becomes that each pianist will rise above his usual level of playing, taxing his powers to the utmost in order to create flashier, more imaginative improvisations. Thus, whether or not a bona-fide winner emerges from this contest is really beside the point—although Waller's commentary makes his judgment in the matter clear. The dialogue itself, beginning over Duncan's solo, proceeds as follows:

Waller:	Aw, that's Brother Duncan; he's gettin' smart, too. Hear that cat stridin' over there? Looks like he's tryin' to get something from me.
(Voices in background)	
Unidentified band member:	He's after you!
Waller:	Looks like he's trying to get something from me.
(Voices in background—occasional)	
Unidentified band member:	Show him how to swing, Hanky!
Waller:	Aw, I ain't gonna have that. Aw, I got him some—he belongs to me! He's *mine!*
Band member:	Go get it!

Waller: He's *mine!* There he is—turn it loose!

(Waller begins his solo)

Waller: Hah, hah! Well, *all* right!

(The "he" Waller refers to at the beginning of the dialogue is obviously Duncan; however, Waller's triumphant shouts of "he's *mine*" at the close of Duncan's solo suggest that the pronoun now is intended to designate the music itself, and that Waller already knows he will win before he has played a note. This personification of the music is particularly unequivocal in his final comment—"there he is"—uttered just before he begins his solo, as if he could at that very moment envision in a corporeal way the solo he is about to perform. Waller's "turn it loose" seems less to belong to the preceding dialogue than simply to prompt the start of his solo, as if, like the athlete who requires proper timing at the beginning of a race, he needs some form of the "on your marks—get set—go" cadence to help start him off at precisely the right moment.)

The cutting contest provides an opportunity to compare Duncan's and Waller's stride directly. Duncan's solo, although simple in terms of the technical rigor of his gestures, is nevertheless rewarding in some ways. Its rhythm is understated but lively, and Duncan's touch is both sure and delicate. His first eight-measure phrase contains little more than a steady (but fast) stride bass and a straightforward series of right-hand chords articulated primarily on strong beats. In the second eight-measure phrase, Duncan substitutes in the left hand a brief descending line in octaves for the stride bass in alternate measures, and limits the use of his right hand to a single four-note gesture that appears at the end of each two-measure group. For the bridge, he suspends the use of the left hand altogether, outlining several two-measure arpeggios with his right hand. And finally, for the last eight-measure phrase, Duncan repeats his material from the opening phrase, closing with a few chords played on strong beats.

Where Duncan is understated, Waller is exuberant, extroverted and energetic. He tears into his solo with a cleanly articulated double trill in thirds ("There he is!")—a bravura, rapid-fire gesture that constitutes his opening salvo in the contest. His left hand strides confidently; the thumb accents the upper note of each tenth, creating a simple but effective melodic line in the tenor range which descends by half-steps. Thus Waller introduces an element of counterpoint into his playing that animates his solo from the beginning. The first phrase closes with Waller leading up to a conventional $I^{6/4}$–V–I cadence by outlining, in octaves played by the left hand, a strongly articulated descent by half steps, while his right hand breaks the trill with a syncopated line that curves down to the tonic. As if to reemphasize his technical supremacy, he then repeats this boldly characterized phrase without change and without error. For the bridge, Waller uses the original tune, but stretches it out, striking each pitch on the beat and eliminating the syncopated profile of the original. Waller's left hand continues to stride in tenths until the last two measures of the phrase. There he abandons the original completely, preparing for a return to the tonic (B*b* major) by again using octaves in the left hand to descend through a scale. But then, in the most daring gesture of the whole improvisation, Waller suspends all action: the tonic never arrives. The scale, descending an octave from the F below middle C, ends on the last beat of the bridge's final measure, and Waller, at the very moment we would expect him to launch into a newly improvised statement of the opening phrase, simply holds that final dominant pitch, F. The rhythm section continues to articulate the beat, of course, but because Waller has stopped playing, we are momentarily disoriented—without the tune to guide us, we can't easily establish where we are in the phrase. Hitherto, Waller has packed a substantial amount of rhythmic and melodic activity into his solo. Now, the abrupt and total cessation of all action in the piano, combined with the sustained dominant, functions as a powerful means of arousing expectancy in the listener.

To break the mounting tension, Waller abandons his customary sophistication and technical agility altogether and slams his whole hand (or possibly even his arm) down on the keys twice in the new phrase (on the first beat of the second measure, and the fourth beat of the third measure). It is as if he can only vent his uncontrollable enthusiasm by turning the piano into a percussion instrument. Thus far in the contest he has already demonstrated his superior prowess as a stride pianist; now, caught up in the vitality of his own playing, and perhaps frustrated by not being able to get enough sound out of the piano to satisfy the aesthetic demands of this climactic moment, in spite of his technique, he finds only one solution—the simplest and most unexpected gesture of all. And then, just as suddenly as it had been created, the tension is gone. Waller demonstrates that, after all, he remains in control of his musical ideas and his technique; in the second half of the phrase, he reestablishes a swinging stride bass that supports a polished right-hand gesture to conclude the solo.

The 4 December 1935 recording of "I Got Rhythm" demonstrates that Waller continued to consolidate his strengths as an improviser while introducing new and arresting ideas into his playing. It is ironic, therefore, that his increased control over the various elements of his style during this period apparently obscured his creative powers as a jazz soloist for some critics.

The splendid ease with which Waller could now produce one accomplished performance after another created, in the final analysis, the misleading impression that his later improvisations lacked freshness and originality.

"I Ain't Got Nobody"

The basic components of Waller's language remained intact during the latter half of the 1930s, but we can also discern a new subtlety in his playing—in effect, the incursion of an introspective atmosphere into his hitherto consistently energetic and boisterous style. This new tone is marked by a preference for uncomplicated gestures, for longer and more straightforward melodic lines, for less florid ornamentation, for chromatic or unpredictable harmonic sequences, and for a simple and understated stride bass. Perhaps most startling in these performances is the complete absence of satire. Waller's playing, even at its most reflective, is much too whimsical ever to be characterized as sober or humorless; nevertheless, I sense a tone of seriousness in these later conceptions that precludes burlesque and parody—a seriousness defined by the frequent use of legato phrasing, an elegant and gentle swing, a refined touch, slower tempi, and a more lyrical approach to melody.

One gauge of the strength of this new development in Waller's playing can be found in the performances of the Roger Graham/Spencer Williams song "I Ain't Got Nobody"[6] recorded on 6 March 1935 and on 11 June 1937. The opening piano solos for both the vocal and instrumental versions of 6 March (matrix numbers 88777-1 and 88778-1, respectively) demonstrate that the basic vocabulary of Waller's improvisations remained grounded in stride technique, but that his playing style had been clearly influenced by the rhetoric of swing. Waller sets an upbeat tempo (approximately ♩ = 90), a pace that already suggests that he is unable to take seriously the mournful, self-pitying message of the text embodied in the title. In the version recorded two years later, however (matrix number 010656-1), Waller's approach to the interpretation of this song is entirely different. The tempo is exactly half that of the 1935 takes, an indication that Waller here intends to dignify rather than satirize the sentiment of the text. The new tempo also allows him to experiment with a wider variety of expressive possibilities.

The 1937 version involves only a four-measure introduction and two thirty-two-measure (AABA) choruses in contrast to the longer structure of the 1935 versions. Waller's relaxed pace and delicate touch define from the outset the introspective quality that distinguishes this performance from its predecessors. But the first two eight-measure phrases (mm. 5–20) provide

even more striking evidence of Waller's new approach. Instead of using a
stride bass pattern, Waller improvises a lightly swinging countermelody for
the left hand. The right hand plays the tune's original melody, but in a reversal of usual roles, the right hand also provides the chords, in effect "comping"
(in jazz parlance, accompanying with block chords) for the left hand's more
active melodic line. Consistent with this reversal, Waller maintains a subdued, mezzo-piano dynamic level for the right hand while bringing the left
hand's melodic line into greater prominence.

Waller's improvisation accomplishes three aesthetic purposes simultaneously. First, the active melodic line in the bass and tenor range acts as a foil
for the staid progress of the original melody in the right hand. (Waller injects
a bit of energy into the right-hand melody in the second eight-measure
phrase [Example 4.1, mm. 13–16] by starting on the pitch A, a minor third
below the first pitch of the original tune [C]. This substitution necessitates a
jump upwards to C midway through the measure in order to begin the tune
in a recognizable form. Thus the right hand outlines a melodic profile that,
like the left hand's, moves upward, albeit in a vastly simplified form.) Second,

Example 4.1

the predominant [rhythmic figure] rhythmic pattern of the countermelody imparts a sense of swing and forward motion to the phrase. Third, by
lightly accenting the E♭ and B♭ in measure 13 (see Example 4.1), Waller
creates an arresting imbalance in the vertical sonority at those moments.
The E♭ and B♭ constitute respectively the flatted seventh degree of the

scale (traditionally considered a "blue" note in jazz) and the fourth degree of the scale. A flatted seventh is not in and of itself a particularly unusual pitch to discover in a melodic line of this kind, but as an accented, syncopated blue note incorporated into a melody played in the tenor range of the piano by the left hand, it is. At the point where the E*b* appears, the tonic harmony (F major), which at the beginning of the measure had been unequivocally stated, suddenly loses its sharp focus; it fades from view even further when Waller strikes the B*b*, a pitch essentially unrelated to any sonority in the measure. Furthermore, the articulation of these two pitches at the very end of the second and fourth beats heightens the syncopation of the phrase. And since both pitches are held over into the following beats, the countermelody as a whole projects a gently lurching quality: it is off balance rhythmically as well as harmonically. Although this activity subsides in measure 14, the second measure of the phrase, where Waller outlines a straightforward, on-the-beat chromatic descent, it is resurrected in measure 15.

Other gestures throughout the performance amplify the sense of expectations denied that characterizes Waller's new introspective voice. Wherever stride bass appears, it is delicately played; Waller's deft touch and detached articulation deemphasize the pattern's inherent bounce and angularity at this slow tempo. (Even where he briefly repeats chords deep in the bass in a rhythmic pattern, he minimizes the accentuation of the beat.) At the end of the first bridge phrase (m. 27), Waller tosses off an upward glissando; for the second bridge phrase, he repeats and extends this gesture by returning back down to the center of the keyboard (mm. 59–60). Because he articulates both sweeps clearly and evenly, without changing dynamic level, he dissipates rather than heightens sonoral energy.

Halfway through the second phrase of the second chorus (mm. 48–50), Waller abandons the preexisting tune, inserting a simple rising chromatic line of parallel sixths (Example 4.2). In one sense, this line simply constitutes a slower form of glissando—a more deliberate version of the same musical

Example 4.2

idea. Yet we might also see in the series of rising sixths the harmonic equivalent of an extended passage of syncopation: in the latter, we lose track of
the regular succession of strong and weak beats, and we experience a sense
of mounting tension until the regular pattern is reestablished. With Waller's
chromatically rising line, we lose track of the harmonic pattern of the song,
and the tension mounts—particularly in this passage, where we cannot pre-
dict when it will come to an end—until we get our harmonic bearings back in
measure 50.

At the end of the performance (mm. 65–68), Waller uses a different kind
of repetitive pattern to create an effect related to that of the rising chromatic
line of measures 48–50. Unlike the rising series of sixths, however, this pattern (Example 4.3) does not obscure the harmonic progressions; the stride
bass provides an unequivocal outline of the move to a cadence on the tonic,
F major. Rather, Waller in this instance apparently intends to suspend the
listener's sense of forward motion in the melodic line itself by repeating the
same six-note pattern over a regular stride bass, but offsetting the pattern
by one eighth note so that five eighth notes instead of all six equal one half
note, and articulating it in a slightly uneven gait—a rhythm impossible to
notate precisely. Without the rhythmic displacement and subtle unevenness,
this device would amount to little more than another in the vast stride vocabulary of gestures for the right hand. With them, however, Waller produces
an aimless, meandering melodic figure instead of the definitive statement of
the original melody we might anticipate at the song's conclusion. Thus for

Example 4.3

the third time in this performance of "I Ain't Got Nobody," our expectations remain unfulfilled and our sense of balance is disturbed. In developing his new introspective approach, then, Waller avoids the virtuoso display that often marks his earlier improvisations. He demonstrates instead a different and more profound kind of agility by manipulating the musical material of his improvisations in unexpected but related (and hence, unifying and aesthetically satisfying) ways.

"Inside (This Heart of Mine)"

Perhaps no other set of alternate takes offers such convincing proof of Waller's extraordinarily fertile musical imagination in its introspective phase than the two solo piano statements of the eight-measure introduction of "Inside (This Heart of Mine)" (words by J. C. Johnson, music by Waller) recorded 12 April 1938 (matrix numbers 022436-1 and 022436-2; Examples 4.4 and 4.5). The stark simplicity of design evident in both statements is complemented by the coherent motivic approach to the improvisation of a melodic line that marks all of Waller's best work. Furthermore, Waller uses a highly sophisticated and advanced harmonic idiom in both passages, quite unlike anything in his recorded work prior to this time. Yet the two statements differ in almost every other respect—in phrase construction and in pace and direction of harmonic motion, for example, as well as in melodic profile and details of melodic motives. The only common ties between them are the key, C minor, and their length. Thus, even in a pair of excerpts this brief— excerpts based on the same source and recorded at the same session—we find ample and convincing evidence that Waller did not base his improvisations in the performances of the late 1930s on preconceived formulas, but created highly individual statements spontaneously out of the same material. And as with "I Ain't Got Nobody," more than the actual musical material itself is involved; Waller's conceptions encompass all aspects of his execution of the piece—touch, phrasing, accent, dynamics.

Example 4.4

The opening two measures of take one of "Inside (This Heart of Mine)" project C minor as the tonic key, although that projection is somewhat tentative, since Waller doesn't place the tonic pitch (C) in the root (i.e., bottom) position, but uses instead the first inversion position of the C minor chord with E♭ at the bottom. But this positioning of the chord facilitates the delicate oscillation between C minor and the seventh chord on D in measures 1–2 of Example 4.4. Each of these harmonies lasts two beats in both measures. The right hand, using the high treble register, outlines the interval of a fifth, descending through the tonic minor triad from G to C in two different rhythmic configurations. Suddenly, in measure 3, Waller shifts to a new, unexpected harmony that bears no real functional relationship to the tonic.[7] This new harmony is defined both by the interval of a minor seventh (C#-B) outlined by the left hand, and by the descending decorative figure in the right hand. Because it lacks any identifiable fundamental pitch, it seems suspended in the texture: it is neither the goal of any clearly recognizable harmonic progression, nor does it function as a particular step in such a progression. Rather, it is a passing sonority, and Waller underscores its transient nature by repeating the gesture in its entirety twice, each time transposing it down a half step (mm. 3–4).

Waller alters the chromatic stepwise pattern of this descent in the second half of measure 4, but retains the essential character of the gesture, maintaining its function (that of a passing chord), its length (one half note), and its general shape (minor seventh in the left hand, descending figure in the right hand). He then slows the pace of harmonic motion in measure 5, lingering for a whole measure on the same sonority (now based on a minor seventh chord built on F and E♭) while outlining a slightly altered and extended version of the right hand's figure. This revised version of the gesture is then repeated up a half step in measure 6 before the left hand subsides in measure 7 to the previous seventh chord on F and E♭, now colored by the addition of A-natural. As in measures 1 and 2 of the introduction, then, Waller again oscillates between two sonorities whose lowest pitches are only a half step apart. The parallel between measures 1–2 and 5–7 is strengthened by similarities in the right-hand gestures in both places (e.g., the offbeat inception and descending shape of the two figures).

In measure 7, however, Waller introduces a new figure in the right hand: a series of triplets constructed on the pitches of a whole tone scale. Of all the different kinds of scales out of which harmonic progressions can be fashioned, the whole tone scale has the least sense of tonal center, of pull toward a position of repose. Waller's gentle, even, and detached articulation of the triplets takes further advantage of the possibilities for tonal drifting inherent in this scale.[8] And in the final measure of the introduction (m. 8), he simply stops on the last pitch of the descending sequence defined by the first note of each triplet (E♭–D♭–C♭–A), as if arrested in midair with, as rock-and-roll artist Chuck Berry suggested in a different context, "no particular place to go." Only on the last beat of measure 8 and the first beat of measure 9—the very last moment possible—does Waller give us some indication of the final harmonic destination of the introduction by striking individually first G and then C deep in the bass register. This motion implies a dominant-tonic cadence in the key of C minor, the key in which the piece began.

Ordinarily, and especially in the Tin Pan Alley genre, one might expect an introduction to define the important musical signposts of the song that follows, and no signpost could be more crucial to a song's ambience than its key. Why, then, is Waller at such pains, not merely to disguise the tonic, but essentially to ignore it? Why does he create such an extensive passage of harmonic dislocation, when one of the principal functions of an introduction should be to identify the central key area of the piece? The opening lines of text may well provide a clue: "Outside it's sunny, but in this heart of mine, / The world is gloomy, the sun refuse' to shine." In developing the drifting, unstable sequence of harmonies that permeates the introduction, Waller seeks to evoke the inner world depicted in the song's opening couplet. The despair of that world proceeds from the situation of the song's narrator: cut off from his lover, he lacks one of life's emotional anchors. (The final line of the song, "Love is a stranger inside this heart of mine," poetically underscores his loss.) Hence, Waller's introduction progresses without any sense of harmonic direction or overall tonic identity.

It is nothing short of astonishing, therefore, that Waller, to evoke the same situation in the second take, devises a harmonic plan based on exactly the opposite musical principle. In take two, the first six measures of the introduction are constructed over a pedal point on C, firmly grounding the piece in the key of C minor. (If Waller had performed this improvisation on the organ, he would have held down the pitch C on the pedalboard for a full six measures.) Thus, no ambiguity over the tonal center of the piece ever

Example 4.5

arises; Waller regularly returns to some manifestation of the C minor chord on the downbeats of every other measure—measures 3, 5, and 7. In addition, as if to stress that the principal concept inherent in this improvisation was that of cyclical structure as opposed to spontaneity, Waller doggedly repeats the same basic harmonic pattern over two measure groups—measures 3–4 and 5–6 (Example 4.6).

Example 4.6

As opposed, then, to the unpredictable harmonic shifts in take one, Waller imposes a tight harmonic coherence on the introduction to take two, unifying the passage further through the unrelenting ♩♩♩ rhythmic pattern of the line and the consistent use of only one texture—two-part counterpoint. (We should recall here that this notation in Waller's playing actually stands for ♩♪♩♪ .)

This high degree of internal unity and harmonic consistency does not mean, however, that Waller has abandoned chromatic elaboration as an expressive device. On the contrary, in spite of the insistent pedal point, Waller freely introduces several effective touches of chromatic decoration. These range from brief moments, such as the last beat of the first measure, where he strikes an E and D simultaneously in the left hand, but releases the E while holding the D over the bar line, to longer gestures, for example, the harmonic progression cooked up for measures 7 and 8. By the first beat of measure 7, Waller has already arrived at his destination, C minor, through a dominant-tonic cadence; he then has two full measures open before him in which to improvise. Almost as if to negate the harmonic constancy of the previous six measures—that is, as if to demonstrate that within the space of the introduction he can engage in both chromatic decoration of the melodic line and chromatic elaboration of the harmonic plan—he glides into a chord (a triad on G*b*) as far removed from the tonic (C minor) as possible, and just as deftly returns to the dominant seventh chord (G major) at the end of measure 8 in preparation for the restatement of the tonic at the beginning of measure 9. We should note, too, that this rapid and fluent shift is accomplished without ever abandoning the omnipresent and characteristic ♩♪ ♩. ♪ rhythmic pattern of this passage, thus linking the closing measures to the introduction as a whole.

In take two of "Inside (This Heart of Mine)," then, Waller supplements the pervasive C minor harmony with an angular, jerky melody, with the open hollow sound of two lines widely separated on the piano's keyboard, and even with the unpredictable timing of the repeated articulation of the C in the bass to create an appropriately despondent atmosphere. Although there are some shared attributes between the introductions for takes one and two—the soft dynamic level and Waller's delicate touch, for example—each offers its own separate logic to express the narrator's melancholy. The basic plans Waller devises to illustrate the sense of the song's text are quite different in the two passages, and collectively, they provide dramatic evidence that his powers of improvisation remained strong and supple, in spite of the taxing demands that had been made on them during the course of this decade.

"I Can't Give You Anything But Love"

Waller's introspective approach to improvisation continued to have an effect on much of his playing in the recording studio—not just on individual passages or isolated gestures, but occasionally on entire conceptions. The two versions of "I Can't Give You Anything But Love" (words by Dorothy Fields, music by Jimmy McHugh) Waller recorded on 3 November 1939 (matrix numbers 043351-1 and 043351-2) suggest that he could be equally at ease satirizing a song or treating it seriously, even at the same recording session. (These two versions should not be confused with the recording of the same song Waller made over a year earlier with Adelaide Hall, on his first trip to London on 28 August 1938.) The lyrics of this ditty are representative of their genre—sentimental and artificial, clever in incorporating contemporary allusions, but not particularly profound in terms of emotional impact. As such, we could expect that they would provide grist for Waller's satiric mill. Indeed, in the first take, with vocal solos by Una Mae Carlisle and himself, Waller consistently responds to almost every phrase sung by Carlisle with a remark designed to destroy any semblance of sincerity in the performance. In all probability, the preconceived arrangement for this take would have stipulated a vocal solo of the complete lyric for Carlisle accompanied by Waller and the ensemble, followed by a Waller vocal solo on the same text; this contrast would have incorporated an interpretation of the text from a feminine as well as from its originally masculine point of view. If such a scheme represented the original arrangement, however, Waller didn't keep to it— not surprisingly, given his penchant for savaging lyrics that expressed similarly banal sentiments. Thus, when Carlisle sings "Gee, I love to see you lookin' swell, baby," Waller interjects in the pause after the word "swell" in Carlisle's line, "Well, my tailor's waitin' right outside the door [—now you can get me lookin' swell—I ain't plain]." He doesn't even permit Carlisle to finish her line before interrupting. His own vocal solo is likewise punctuated with satiric jabs, emendations, and even the sly suggestion of an epithet, thrown in for heightened comic relief. (Waller changes the original line "Diamond bracelets Woolworth's doesn't sell, baby" to "Diamond bracelets— Woolworth ain't got no business sellin' 'em—you can go to—go to—ah well, ah well, well, well.")

In sum, it is a typically witty Waller vocal interpretation. The emphasis on the verbal satire, however, comes at the expense of Waller's playing; there is, except for the somewhat banal introduction, no piano solo at all, and Waller keeps his accompanying well in the background for both Carlisle's vocal and his own. Like the contrast between the two introductions to "Inside (This Heart of Mine)," however, the introduction and opening piano solo of take two of "I Can't Give You Anything But Love"[9] projects an atmosphere entirely removed from that of take one, and therefore comes as something of an aural shock (Example 4.7). Not only has Waller eliminated any trace of satire or even humor from his playing, but he has also transformed the original rather uninteresting melodic material into an improvised statement highly rhapsodic in character.

Example 4.7

How the opening gesture of the introduction (m. 1) strikes the listener might depend on whether one knows the song. If the amiable melody and easygoing swing of the original opening line are firmly fixed in one's mind, then Waller's angular, dissonant opening—in a *minor* key, no less—with its jagged rhythms and syncopation jolts one's aesthetic system. On the other hand, even if one didn't know the tune (an unlikely possibility for a 1939 audience, since the song had been composed over a decade earlier and performed and recorded often), Waller's introduction suggests a rather more disquieting atmosphere than that implied by the lyrics. In either case, Waller's manipulation of the harmony—his use of the same kind of aimless, free-floating chromatic descent apparent in the first take of "Inside (This Heart of Mine)"—again produces an aural disorientation. In a sense, the listener, freed from the pull of a preconceived and perceptible harmonic pattern that would have prepared the opening of the song by identifying the tonic key, concentrates on the gesture of the moment, on each new harmonic and melodic twist. We follow the exquisite detail so carefully because Waller has obscured the existence of a definite plan. Thus, we endure a certain amount of heightened anticipation during this passage, a sensation that gives way to one of startling recognition when the tune itself first appears.

Waller himself must have been sensitive to that experience of recognition, because the statement of the tune's two opening phrases, which immediately follows the introduction (m. 5–8 and 9–12), is generally straightforward. In the second half of each of these phrases, however, Waller abandons the thematic material of the tune: he closes the first phrase (m. 7–8) with a shower of descending thirty-second notes, a gesture that typically appears at similar junctures, and he concludes the second phrase (m. 11–12) with a meandering line, continuing the dotted rhythmic pattern of the introduction. This meandering line becomes the genesis of a new improvisatory idea in which the primary melodic gestures are centered in the octave below middle C (the piano's tenor register), while the stride accompaniment continues around them. And when Waller comes to the end of this phrase, the third four-measure group of the melody (mm. 13–16), he suddenly jumps almost three octaves to continue the melodic line (Example 4.8). The effect is capricious but oddly satisfying; the upward leap itself is unexpected, but the sound of the new high register complements that of the tenor range exploited in the previous phrase. Waller provides a further connection between the two phrases as well by employing in both of them gestures for the right hand that incorporate descending thirds.

This rich variety of gesture pervades Waller's piano solo in the second take. And although he launches a few satiric barbs in his interpretation of the

Example 4.8

lyrics, he sings in a far more subdued manner than on the first take, in keeping with the delicacy of his improvisations. From a purely musical point of view, then, Victor's failure to issue the second take, which on its own and very different terms is as rewarding a version as the first take, is indefensible. Waller's manager, Ed Kirkeby, may have calculated that the duet, with its barrage of vocal banter between Waller and Carlisle, would have a greater immediate appeal, and hence greater commercial value than the version by Waller alone. In making such judgments on this and other recordings, Kirkeby, although he helped to improve Waller's financial situation considerably, may inadvertently have diminished for a time Waller's reputation as a jazz pianist.[10] Certainly, because recorded performances that offered telling evidence of Waller's abilities as an improviser were often kept out of circulation, Waller's image was consistently skewed toward that of a popular entertainer. But on those occasions when Waller decided to employ a slow tempo, as he did in the unissued performances we have just examined, he could use his superlative technique to highly original aesthetic ends.

In the final analysis, Waller's early mastery of the elements of stride—a secure, steady, and accurate left hand, and an exceptionally broad vocabulary of gestures for the right hand—coupled with a fertile musical imagination, provided him with the means to create fresh improvisations and to execute them flawlessly. As he became a more experienced pianist, these capabilities increased, in part because of and in part in spite of the often hectic pace of his career. At his best, Waller transformed his material into powerful and compelling musical statements. The processes he used—melodic embellishment, rhythmic displacement, chromatic elaborations, structural manipulation, and others—are essentially compositional in nature. As such, they contrast with a more orthodox kind of stride in which preconceived gestures or "tricks" are imposed on a melodic and harmonic framework in order to demonstrate an individual pianist's superiority (i.e., technical agility) as a performer.

But even when the material he was given to record was uninspiring, or when the circumstances under which he had to record worked to his disadvantage, Waller always turned in at the very least a competent (and not uninteresting) performance. Often, in fact, careful examination of these "competent" performances reveals subtle but telling alterations that ultimately enrich the original material. Waller's version of "Stayin' at Home" (words by Andy Razaf, music by Waller), for example, recorded relatively late in his career on 16 July 1940 (matrix no. 051870-1), demonstrates that he enhances even his most straightforward playing with details that confirm his consummate skill as a pianist and jazz musician. He gently states the opening piano solo, creating an atmosphere of deceptive ease that belies the extent of his technical and musical control. He makes use of a stride bass, but subjects it to numerous subtle variations: at one point, he vacillates delicately between a minor ii chord on D and the dominant seventh of the dominant, also on D, shifting from one to the other on each beat (Example 4.9).

Example 4.9

The ornamentation of the melodic line is spare, even perfunctory, until the end of the passage, when Waller suddenly breaks away from the melody in order to repeat a short four-note descent several times. He incorporates minute shifts in rhythmic accentuation and in texture (for example, the octave doubling he lends the third phrase). And of course, he infuses the whole with impeccable swing. Such unassuming but elegant playing substantiates again that Waller's genius had an unexpected, introspective side.

More than five years before Waller recorded "Stayin' at Home," other musicians who had started their careers as stride pianists like Waller, notably Count Basie and Art Tatum, had already begun to evolve their own unique contributions to the history of jazz piano, contributions rooted in the fertile soil of stride, but branching out in new directions. It seems unlikely that Waller would have expanded further or changed his own language in order to keep pace with these contemporary developments; in his recordings, at least, he seems to have made no effort to adapt his technique to the new styles. Yet there exists testimony beyond that of the recordings that assures us that Waller's was a broadly educated as well as a sensitive mind; Andy Razaf, his longtime collaborator and lyricist, remarked in a reminiscence published shortly after Waller's death:

I don't think people realize what great depth there was in Fats. He knew Brahms, Liszt and Beethoven as well as he knew jazz, and often discussed and analyzed their work. He was well read, too; he read and talked about Shakespeare and Plato and could have been a great actor. [11]

And I find it difficult to believe that such a prodigious and prolific musical intelligence as Waller's would not in some way have approached and absorbed some of the developments of the middle and late 1940s. Gene Sedric, Waller's saxophonist, also reported that the scope of Waller's talent was generally underestimated by his public:

> [Fats] was appreciated for his showmanship ability and for that amount of piano that he played on records, but very few of Waller's record fans knew how much more he could play than what he usually did on records. . . . Yet he wanted to do great things on organ and piano—which he could do. There were many times when we played engagements during which he felt like himself and wanted to play great. But when he played as musically as he could, many people in the audience would think that he was lying down. . . . He could play all styles from modern on down. What is generally called the Waller style is more or less the style he became known by commercially. He had a much wider range than most people realize.[12]

Thus, perhaps Waller was already fluent in the more advanced (and more stylish) practices of his younger contemporaries. Perhaps at after-hours sessions, away from the demands of a live performance or a recording studio, he proved the continued vitality of his own playing, constantly improving and expanding his powers. Perhaps, had he lived a few more decades, his reputation would again have become that of a jazz pianist of major significance. Yet in the end, Waller's own voice obtrudes with gentle irony upon these speculations with the final word about what might have been: "One never knows, do one?"

Appendix

Estey Pipe Organ (opus 2370)

**Specification for a three manual pipe organ with Pedals
Compass of Manuals CC to C 4, 61 Notes
Compass of Pedals CCC to G, 32 Notes**

NAME OF STOP	PITCH
Great Organ:	
Major Open Diapason (New)	8 ft.
First Open Diapason	8 ft.
Second Open Diapason	8 ft.
Major Flute (New)	8 ft.
Flute	8 ft.
Gamba	8 ft.
Gemshorn	8 ft.
Viol d'Orchestre	8 ft.
Viol Celeste (New)	8 ft.
Flute	4 ft.
Flute Harmonic (New)	4 ft.
Oboe	8 ft.
Cornopean (New in place of trumpet)	8 ft.
Clarinet	8 ft.
Saxophone	8 ft.
Vox Humana	8 ft.

Swell Organ:
All stops duplexed from Great, with the addition of Tremolo

Solo Organ:	
Stentorphone (New)	8 ft.
Tibia Plena (New)	8 ft.
Gross Gamba (New)	8 ft.

Gamba Celeste (New)	8 ft.
First Violin (New)	III Ranks
Flute (New)	4 ft.
Piccolo Harmonic (New)	2 ft.
Orchestral Oboe (New)	8 ft.
Tuba Profunda (New)	16 ft.
Tuba (New)	8 ft.
Clarion (New)	4 ft.

Pedal Organ:

Open Diapason (New)	16 ft.
Bourdon (New)	16 ft.
Bass Viol	8 ft.
Trombone	16 ft.
Tuba	8 ft.

Notes and References

Chapter 1

The title of chapter 1 is taken from an aside spoken by Waller on his recording of "Mighty Fine" (matrix no. 044602-1), made on 12 January 1940.

1. To produce a chronology of the Waller family before Thomas's birth, we must rely primarily on the two biographical accounts of Waller's life available: Ed Kirkeby (in collaboration with Duncan P. Schiedt and Sinclair Traill), *Ain't Misbehavin': The Story of Fats Waller* (New York, 1966), and Maurice Waller and Anthony Calabrese, *Fats Waller* (New York, 1977). Information in one account will occasionally supplement information in the other; on certain matters of fact, they may disagree. But most of the disagreements can be reconciled, and by using both accounts, a picture emerges that is probably reasonably accurate. The pertinent information concerning the background of Waller's family appears on pp. 2–6 in Kirkeby and on pp. 1–3 in Waller.

2. Maurice Waller suggests that his father's family settled at 107 West 134th St. "after trying a few apartments" (3). Maurice's account, unlike Kirkeby's, leaves unclear the dates of the family's moves, and is likewise ambiguous concerning the location of Thomas's birth.

3. Kirkeby, *Ain't Misbehavin'*, 11.

4. Although the exact sequence of events of Waller's childhood is somewhat difficult to trace and verify with unimpeachable accuracy, some biographical data seem probable as well as reasonable, even without documentary corroboration. (Again, these data can be inferred from information in both Kirkeby and Waller.)

5. Kirkeby, *Ain't Misbehavin'*, 144; Waller, *Fats Waller*, 95.

6. Charles Fox, in his brief study *Fats Waller* (New York: A. S. Barnes and Co., 1961) disputes the June 1939 date for the composition of "The London Suite." He argues, "The date of 12 June, usually given for the original recording of *The London Suite*, is patently false. A full account of the session, together with a photograph, appeared in the *Melody Maker* on 8 April 1939" (p. 66, note 1). That a recording session took place on 3 April 1939 is certainly true; but according to Rust (*Jazz Records*), the songs recorded on that date were "You Can't Have Your Cake and Eat It," "Not There—Right There," "Cottage in the Rain," and "What a Pretty Miss." Rust indicates further that there were two June sessions in London (12 and 13 June), and the amount of detail provided for the second of these two sessions makes it probable

that 13 June 1939 is, in fact, the date on which *The London Suite* was recorded. (See discography.)

    7. *New York Times,* 21 December 1943, 28.

Chapter 2

    1. Such contests, with their displays of agility and artistry, belong to the traditions of Western European music as well as to those of jazz. One of the most famous historical cutting contests involved Wolfgang Amadeus Mozart and Muzio Clementi, and took place on 24 December 1781 at the court of Joseph II in Vienna. In an interesting parallel to twentieth-century Harlem contests, Mozart and Clementi, in addition to playing compositions in their repertoires and at sight, were required to improvise.

    2. Waller, *Fats Waller,* 21.

    3. Kirkeby, *Ain't Misbehavin',* 24.

    4. Before 1927, Waller had recorded a total of about thirty titles: twenty with blues singers, two piano solos, two organ solos, and six with various groups—two with Fletcher Henderson, two with the Jamaica Jazzers, one with the Six Hot Babies (four rejected takes of "All God's Chillun Got Wings"), and one accompanying the Elkins Negro Ensemble, a chorus.

    5. Waller's ability to transpose easily and fluently is documented in the two versions of "Sugar" he recorded on 20 May, 1927—one as a solo (matrix no. 38044-1) and one accompanying Alberta Hunter (matrix no. 38045-2).

    6. Richard Hadlock, *Jazz Masters of the Twenties* (New York, 1965), 153.

    7. Nat Shapiro and Nat Hentoff, eds., *Hear Me Talkin' to Ya* (New York, 1966), 253.

    8. Ibid., 259.

    9. Ibid., 266–67.

    10. Murray Schumach, "Interviewing Fats Waller and His Piano," *New York Times,* 25 July 1943, section 2, 1 (column 4). Maurice Waller cites this same article on pages 98 and 111 of his biography, but incorrectly identifies the date of the *Times* issue (on 111) as June 25 instead of July 25.

    11. In an interview published in the February 1936 issue of *Metronome* (52, no. 2:19, 33; Richard Hadlock implies the interview was actually held in 1935—see Hadlock, *Jazz Masters,* 153), Waller expands on the role of the left hand:

"Formerly . . . the right hand was given all the work and the other left to shift for itself, thumping out a plain octave or common chord foundation. There was no attempt at figuration. But that is all past. Now it's more evenly divided and the left has to know its stuff, its chords and its figuration just as well as the right. I consider the thorough bass foundation I got in the study of Bach the best part of my training."

Fats studied with Carl Bohm in the Juilliard School in New York and with [Leopold] Godowsky in Chicago. Under Godowsky he went through the Toccatas, and the two and three part inventions of Bach. But when he came to the fugues, Fats rebelled, claiming he did not need them in jazz. He is now arranging one of the two part inventions in D minor for his band using six saxophones, two altos, tenor, baritone and two sopranos.

Fats is all for getting grounded in the classics first not only as a technical preparation, but "whenever you get stuck for a two bar harmonic device, you can always go back to Liszt, or Chopin. Even so, it's all in knowing what to put on the right beat."

Here are some of his precepts. ["]First get a thorough bass. Make it more rhythmic than flashy, a pulsating bass. Know how to play first without pedals and then always use the pedals sparingly. Study harmony so you will know the chords. Play clean both in the right and left hand. This is one of the marks of the modern pianist, he plays much cleaner than the old school. There is also much more expression to modern playing and it is necessary to know how to build climaxes, how to raise up and let down, to show sudden contracts [*sic;* the word intended here is surely *contrasts*]. Keep the right hand always subservient to the melody. Trying to do too much always detracts from the tune.["]]

12. Hadlock, *Jazz Masters,* 153.

13. Often at these early recording sessions, Waller would record the same song two or three times, probably to insure that a performance of the highest caliber would eventually be released. When one of the available takes was selected for pressing, the others would be either discarded or shelved.

14. Jean-Paul Guiter produced two five-disc "Memorial" boxed sets, one in 1969 and one in 1971, which contained a total of 142 of Waller's recordings; both sets were issued by RCA of France. (The second of these retrospectives contains many alternate takes.) Guiter then undertook to reissue all remaining Waller material recorded for Victor, an additional 350 separate takes or so, as well as reissuing the sixteen-inch discs made for Associated Transcriptions (also known as Associated Program Service Recordings and Muzak Associated) and some of his V-discs. (But the producer's claim that no material already issued on the memorial volumes or on previous albums in the series would be duplicated was not quite correct; a number of items in volumes 19, 20, 21, and 22, for example, had been previously issued on the two memorial sets.) For most of these albums, two separate groups of liner notes exist, one in French by Pierre-François Cangardel, and one in English by Roy Cooke. Although there are some important lacunae in this mammoth series of reissues—Waller's work in the 1920s accompanying blues singers, his piano rolls, material from some radio broadcasts, the Lang-Worth transcription discs, sessions recorded with other major artists for other labels, and a few recordings made in England constitute some of the items not included—it is nevertheless the most substantial and complete collection of Waller's recordings currently available.

15. Indeed, examining all the performances made of a particular piece at various stages in Waller's career reveals an even greater depth and intelligence in his playing than documented by multiple takes from one session alone. Such a study establishes with particular clarity stylistic changes which take place over the course

of several years. In other words, comparisons among various versions of the same piece provide us with a uniquely unambiguous set of facts—that is, the different ways Waller plays the same passage—which enable us to follow the growth and development of his style.

16. For the most likely sequence of events, see Waller, *Fats Waller*, 86.

17. Among other distinctions, the song holds the number 8 position (together with "Honeysuckle Rose") on the list of "Top Forty: The Most Often Recorded Songs in America, 1900–1950," compiled by Charles Hamm from information in *The Complete Encyclopedia of Popular Music and Jazz, 1900–1950*, by Roger D. Kinkle (Charles Hamm, *Yesterdays* [New York, 1983], appendix 5, 487).

18. In the 2 August 1929 performance (matrix no. 49492-3), the parallel contour of this left-hand line is unambiguous in the second and fourth eight-measure phrases; in the first phrase, however, Waller's left hand remains in the background, as an accompaniment, and the parallel is not maintained as scrupulously as in the other eight-measure phrases.

19. Waller, *Fats Waller*, 78. Maurice Waller's account of the incident does not indicate either the date or the titles recorded, but since there are only two dates on which Waller recorded with Austin in 1929—26 June and 25 November—the probable date for an incident like this one would be the former, not the latter. (Essentially the same group of musicians played at both sessions.) Also, the session's date suggests that Maurice's anecdote concerning the pivotal role Austin is supposed to have played in engineering Fats Waller's release from jail (Waller, *Fats Waller*, 77) is inaccurate; since Waller played for a session on 1 March 1929, he cannot have been released from jail just prior to the 26 June session. (See Chronology and Discography.)

20. No current discography includes this collaboration between Moore and Waller in its listings and I have been unable to establish its matrix number. But this one recording of them together has been reissued in volume 4 ("The Piano Album") of the Meritt Record Society series of jazz LPs. The first discs in this series were issued in 1980.

21. Waller's accompaniments for blues singer Alberta Hunter in their 1927 recordings, however, are quite different from the 1932 Moore recordings in this respect—that is, less soloistic; a number of factors may have affected the nature of his playing on this earlier occasion. He was not only accompanying Hunter, but he was also recording additional solo pipe organ versions of the same tunes, and in 1927 he had not yet had opportunities to record with a variety of ensembles.

22. Kirkeby, *Ain't Misbehavin'*, 144–45; Waller, *Fats Waller*, 95. The band included, among other luminaries, Benny Goodman. This was, then, the second occasion on which Waller and Goodman recorded together.

23. Kirkeby, *Ain't Misbehavin'*, 149.

24. See Gunther Schuller's discussion of Smith's vocal expertise: *Early Jazz* (New York, 1968), 229–30.

25. Prof. Morroe Berger's article "Fats Waller: The Outside Insider," *Journal of Jazz Studies* 1, no. 1 (Fall 1973):3–20, provides a penetrating and thorough analysis

of Waller's manipulation of song lyrics. It is also one of the very few pieces of intelligent and literate criticism on Waller in print.

26. On 20 November 1939, Waller made several sixteen-inch Lang-Worth transcription discs. The repertoire included on these recordings was somewhat out of the ordinary for Waller: In addition to the spirituals, he played folksongs ("Frankie and Johnny," "She'll be Comin' Round the Mountain" [matrix no. 043186-1]) and piano transcriptions—jazz versions, of course—of excerpts from several operas, among them *Faust* (matrix no. 043189-1), *Lucia di Lammermoor* (matrix no. 043187-1), and *Cavalleria Rusticana* (matrix no. 043188-1).

27. Note that this process, while probably based on an old vaudeville technique of substituting a sophisticated, multisyllabic term for a simple one (in which, for example, "Show me the way to go home" becomes "Indicate the way to my abode"), is quite different: Waller's substitutions alter or reverse the meaning of the original text rather than simply reinforce it, even though nominally the substitutions are synonyms for the words they replace.

28. Other versions of "I'm Crazy 'bout My Baby" recorded by Waller (11 March 1935 [no matrix number]; 1 August 1936 [matrix no. 102400-1]; 7 August 1939 [no matrix number]) confirm that he did not simply repeat an earlier version of the song, as if he were playing composed instead of improvised music. There are, to be sure, some superficial resemblances among the various recordings, but such similarities stem mostly from the use of stride gestures, a characteristic to be expected from a stride musician.

Chapter 3

1. On some organs, this connection is mechanical rather than electrical. In Waller's day, such instruments were primarily historical and of European manufacture.

2. The harmonium, a small reed organ sometimes referred to as a parlor organ, probably graced some black churches and middle-class homes, but it would have been much less common than the piano. In any case, it is a fundamentally different instrument from the pipe organ, and cannot be considered a substitute for it.

3. The correspondence is in the Bailey/Howe Library of the University of Vermont. I am very grateful to Connell Gallagher, Curator of Manuscripts at the Library, for having provided me with copies of the correspondence.

4. From about 1938 on, Waller occasionally played the electric organ, as distinct from the pipe organ, in his Victor recordings, both with his group (Fats Waller and His Rhythm) and as a soloist.

5. In black folk music, the piano has been viewed basically as a rhythmic and percussive instrument. Indeed, in certain genres of black folk music, performers sought to enhance its percussive qualities: barrel-house pianists, for example, put tacks in the hammers, resulting in a sharp, twangy sound when the string was struck.

6. Shapiro and Hentoff, *Hear Me Talkin'*, 266.

7. Ibid.

8. Kirkeby, *Ain't Misbehavin'*, 70.

9. Brian Rust, *Jazz Records, 1897–1942*, 5th revised and enlarged ed. (Chigwell, n.d. [1982]), 1622.

10. Liner notes to RCA 741.052, "Young Fats at the Organ."

11. James J. Fuld, *The Book of World-Famous Music* (New York, 1971), 285. Other sources vary the attribution of words and music somewhat: Kinkle, in *The Complete Encyclopedia of Popular Music and Jazz, 1900–1950*, suggests that the words are by Roger Graham and Dave Peyton, and that the music is by Spencer Williams (1:82); David Ewen, in *American Popular Songs*, suggests that the words are by Roger Graham alone and that the music is by Spencer Williams and Dave Peyton (156). Fuld, however, traces the rather tortuous history of the copyright for "I Ain't Got Nobody" in great detail, and is probably the most authoritative source for this kind of information.

It is worth stressing, I think, that the piano solo performance of "I Ain't Got Nobody" recorded by Waller on 11 June 1937 is an entirely different interpretation of the song, as we will see in chapter 4, as are the two group takes of 6 March 1935. Waller's style had advanced considerably during the decade that separates the earlier and later performances, as the harmonic and rhythmic subtleties of the solo piano version demonstrate. And, as we have already discovered, many of the gestures idiomatic to the piano that Waller frequently employs in improvisations, including the rapidly articulated and lightly pedaled right-hand figuration of the 1937 solo (m. 7–8), for example, are utterly unsuited to the pipe organ, and indeed impossible to achieve on it.

12. Rust, *Jazz Records*, suggests (720) that Waller played pipe organ on "The Chant," recorded with Fletcher Henderson and his orchestra in New York on 3 November 1926. If this were so, it would have constituted Waller's earliest pipe organ/ensemble recording. Two significant objections to this assertion can be raised, however. First, the sound of the instrument on the recording suggests that of a reed organ or harmonium much more closely than it does that of a pipe organ. The sound of a pipe organ might, when reproduced by means of an acoustic recording, resemble that of a reed organ. But the Henderson session was recorded late in 1926; by that time, Columbia, for whom the recording was made, was recording electronically. Not only is the sound that of a reed organ, but Waller's uncharacteristic approach to the instrument—the almost continuous use of block chords, and the absence of any distinctive melodic or rhythmic component—implies an instrument radically different from the pipe organ. Second, although the precise location of the Henderson session is not specified, the New York studio used was probably not equipped with a pipe organ; a reed organ, however, would have been portable enough to have been moved in for the occasion.

13. In the third take of "Won't You Take Me Home" (matrix no. 38052-3), for example, Waller incorporates a driving chromatic run up the scale in triplets in the penultimate blues chorus. The sudden appearance of this dramatic upward rush of sound, played with the full organ, injects a moment of energy and excitement into an otherwise rather staid rendition.

14. Waller, *Fats Waller,* 74.
15. Waller had by this time already made a few other recordings with what was, for jazz, unusual instrumentation. In May 1924 he recorded two sides as pianist for a group called "The Jamaica Jazzers"; the other instruments were percussion and two kazoos. On 17 January 1928 he was part of a violin, cello, and piano trio accompanying vocalist Andy Razaf on two songs recorded for Columbia. (The name Johnny Thompson appears on the Columbia record label as a pseudonym for Razaf.) Then, on 2 and 3 March 1928, Nathaniel Shilkret produced his recordings of the "Rhyth-Melodists"; the group consisted of piano, violin, and organ for the first session and piano, harp, trombone, and organ for the second.
16. Waller also apparently recorded only six songs on which he played pipe organ to accompany his own singing. Four of these, all spirituals, were rejected; the other two, recorded on 13 June 1939 at Waller's last session in London for HMV, reveal only that Waller consistently doubles his vocal line on the organ, taking few improvisational liberties or chances.
17. The solo organ take of "I'm Goin' to See My Ma," (matrix no. 38049-1), the third of the tunes recorded with Hunter, was rejected by Victor; because no extant recording survives, we cannot determine unequivocally that Waller varied its structure from that of the vocal version, but it is nevertheless probable that he did so.
18. This session as a whole must have been quite a marathon, involving a total of eighteen separate takes. It also must have constituted a severe test of Waller's ability to shift from performing intensely serious work to shrewdly satirical, but basically lighthearted, numbers.

Chapter 4

1. Waller's last recording date in 1932 was the session with Monette Moore on 28 September in New York. It is probable, therefore, that he left for Cincinnati after September. (On the other hand, he might have begun his job at WLW earlier in the year, shortly after his 26 July recording session in New York; in this case, the Moore session, which involved only one take, could easily have been arranged and executed while Waller had returned to New York for other purposes.) In any case, there exists, to my knowledge, no documentation of any recordings made by Waller between 28 September 1932 and 16 May 1934, the date of the first "Fats Waller and His Rhythm" sessions for Victor.
2. Albert McCarthy, Alun Morgan, Paul Oliver, and Max Harrison, *Jazz on Record: A Guide to the First 50 Years: 1917–1967* (London, 1968), 297, 298.
3. Interview with Dizzy Gillespie on the CBS Network program "60 Minutes," 13 December 1981.
4. Waller, *Fats Waller,* 114–15:

"Phil [Ponce, Waller's manager at the time] was impressed with the Charlie Turner Band from the Academy of Music and they were retained to work as Dad's band on tour. That group was an impressive one, including Rudy Powell and Don Redman (who also did some of the arrangements) on alto, Gene Sedric and Bob Carroll on tenor, Herman Autrey as one of the trumpeters, Charlie Turner on bass, and Hank Duncan on piano. . . . By the end of 1934 everything was ready and the band was ready to go, but the Victor people wanted Dad for one more recording session before he left New York. On January 5, 1935, the band journeyed to Camden [i.e., to Victor's Camden recording studio]. . . . Once the session was completed Victor said goodbye and the band hit for the road." Maurice implies that Phil Ponce selected the group with which Waller was to perform, and that the musicians were not known to the pianist. However, Waller had already recorded with Sedric and Autrey, and of course, he already knew Hank Duncan. Moreover, of the musicians Maurice lists, only Sedric and Turner are present on the 5 January session. (And the other three musicians on that date—Bill Coleman, Albert Casey, and Harry Dial—had all previously performed with Waller as well.) However, all of the musicians listed by Maurice, with the exception of Don Redman, do participate in the 4 December 1935 recording session. The tour itself, incidentally, must have taken place shortly after that 5 January session, and concluded before 6 March 1935, when Waller was back in the Victor studios (with Autrey, Powell, and Turner, among others) for a long session—thirteen takes.

5. Waller, *Fats Waller,* 115.

6. See chapter 3, note 11.

7. This new chord is rather similar in its construction to a sonority whose name—the "Tristan" chord—derives from the fact that it constitutes a central component of the harmonic vocabulary of the opera *Tristan und Isolde,* composed by Richard Wagner in 1857–1859.

8. Waller uses the whole tone scale in a similar gesture at the beginning of "I'm Gonna Sit Right Down and Write Myself a Letter" (Young/Ahlert) recorded 8 May 1935 (matrix no. 89764-1), but he outlines the scale in a different profile from its appearance in "Inside." He also establishes the tonic harmony unambiguously at the opening of the introduction of "Letter," and we are never in any real doubt as to its identity because the introduction itself is quite brief. Nevertheless, it may not be entirely coincidental that the texts of both songs offer reflections on similar situations.

9. Rust's discography indicates incorrectly that Una Mae Carlisle sings on the second take of "I Can't Give You Anything But Love" (matrix no. 043351-2) as well as on the first (1635).

10. Perhaps, from his point of view, Kirkeby was justified in many of his choices, both of repertoire and of performances to be issued. Certainly Waller's boisterous good humor and bravura technique often produced recordings in the middle to late 1930s that were not merely energetic and entertaining, but often provided some measure of musical interest as well. There are several examples of such recordings, but the following list could be taken as representative:

Dinah (matrix no. 88989-1, 24 June 1935)
I'm on a See-Saw (matrix no. 92998-1, 20 August 1935)
It's a Sin to Tell a Lie (matrix no. 101667-1, 5 June 1936)

Blue, Turning Grey Over You (matrix no. 010651-1, 9 June 1937)
Pantin' in the Panther Room (matrix no. 053797-1, 2 January 1941)

11. Razaf, "Fats Waller," 16.
12. Shapiro and Hentoff, *Hear Me Talkin'*, 264–65.

Selected Bibliography

1. Books (including bibliographies and discographies)

Anderson, Jervis. *This was Harlem: A Cultural Portrait, 1900–1950.* New York: Farrar, Straus & Giroux, 1982.

Charters, Samuel B., and Kunstadt, Leonard. *Jazz: A History of the New York Scene.* Garden City, N.Y.: Doubleday & Co., 1962.

Davies, John R. T. *The Music of Fats Waller.* London: Private printing, [1953].

Ewen, David, ed. *American Popular Songs: From the Revolutionary War to the Present.* New York: Random House, 1966.

Fox, Charles. *Fats Waller.* New York: A. S. Barnes & Co., 1961.

Fuld, James J. *American Popular Music, 1875–1950.* Philadelphia: Musical America, 1956.

————. *The Book of World-Famous Music.* New York: Crown Publishers, 1971.

Hadlock, Richard. *Jazz Masters of the Twenties.* New York: Macmillan, 1965.

Hamm, Charles. *Yesterdays.* New York: Norton, 1983.

Hefele, Bernhard. *Jazz-Bibliographie.* Munich: K. G. Saur Verlag, 1981.

Johnson, James W. *Black Manhattan.* New York: Arno Press, 1968. Reprint of the 1940 edition.

Kinkle, Roger D. *The Complete Encyclopedia of Popular Music and Jazz, 1900–1950.* Westport, Conn.: Arlington House Publishers, 1974.

Kirkeby, Ed (in collaboration with Duncan P. Schiedt and Sinclair Traill). *Ain't Misbehavin': The Story of Fats Waller.* New York: Da Capo, 1975. Unabridged republication of the first edition published by Dodd, Mead & Co., 1966.

Lewis, David Levering. *When Harlem Was in Vogue.* New York: Alfred A. Knopf, 1981.

McCarthy, Albert; Morgan, Alun; Oliver, Paul; and Harrison, Max. *Jazz on Record: A Guide to the First 50 Years: 1917–1967.* London: Hanover Books, 1968.

Meadows, Eddie S. *Jazz Reference and Research Materials: A Bibliography.* New York and London: Garland Publishing, 1981.

Merriam, Alan P., with the assistance of Robert J. Beaford. *A Bibliography of Jazz.* Philadelphia: American Folklore Society, 1954.

Rust, Brian. *Jazz Records, 1897–1942.* 5th revised and enlarged ed. Chigwell, Essex, United Kingdom: Storyville Publications and Co., Ltd., n.d. [1982].

Schuller, Gunther. *Early Jazz. Its Roots and Musical Development.* New York: Oxford University Press, 1968.

Sears, Richard S. *V-Discs. A History and Discography.* Westport, Conn.: Greenwood Press, 1980.

Shapiro, Nat, and Hentoff, Nat, eds. *Hear Me Talkin' to Ya.* New York: Dover Publications, 1966. Reprint of the work originally published by Rinehart & Co., 1955.

Smith, Willie the Lion, with George Hoefer. *Music on My Mind. The Memoirs of an American Pianist.* New York: Da Capo, 1978. Unabridged republication of the first edition published by Doubleday, 1964.

Stratemann, Klaus. *Negro Bands on Film. Volume 1: Big Bands 1928–1950.* Lubbecke: Verlag Uhle & Kleimann, 1981.

Taylor, Billy. *Jazz Piano.* Dubuque: William C. Brown, 1982.

Waller, Maurice, and Calabrese, Anthony. *Fats Waller.* New York: Schirmer Books, 1977.

2. Articles

Bagar, Robert. "Fats Waller in Carnegie Hall." *New York World-Telegram,* 15 January 1942, 14.

Balliett, Whitney. "Jazz: Fats." *New Yorker,* 10 April 1978, 110–17.

Beltonville, Albert. "Fats Waller: Portrait." *Jazz* (Brussels), March 1945, 14.

Berger, Morroe. "Fats Waller: The Outside Insider." *Journal of Jazz Studies* 1, no. 1 (Fall 1973):3–20.

Bright, Kenneth, and Cavanaugh, Inez. "'That Harmful Little Armful': Fats Waller in His Formative Years." *Crisis,* April 1944, 109–10.

Calabrese, Anthony. "He Was the 'Clown' Prince of Jazz." *New York Times,* Sunday, 7 May 1978, section 2, 1, 26.

Cooke, Roy. "The Genius of Thomas Fats Waller." *Jazz Journal,* May 1952, 13.

D[exter], D[ave] E. "Immortals of Jazz." *Downbeat* 8, no. 2 (15 January 1941):10.

Dexter, Dave. "Thomas Waller of Concert Stage Isn't the Mellow Fats of Backroom Jazz." *Downbeat* 9, no. 3 (1 February 1942):3.

Gautier, Madeleine. "Fats Waller." Translated by Walter E. Schaap. *Jazz Hot* 32, nos. 7–8 (July-August 1939):11.

Kogan, Hermann. "Ode to Fats Waller." *Negro Digest* 2 (February 1944):61–62.

L[awrence], R[obert]. "Fats Waller Presents Carnegie Hall Recital." *New York Herald Tribune,* 15 January 1942, 14.

McGraw, James. "Fats Waller and James P." *Jazz Record,* January 1944, 8–9.

Magnusson, Tor. "Fats Waller with Gene Austin on the Record." *Journal of Jazz Studies* 4, no. 1 (Fall 1976):75–83.

Miller, Paul Eduard. "Musical Blasphemies. No. 4: Thomas (Fats) Waller." *Music and Rhythm* 1, no. 6 (April 1941):31.

Panassié, Hugues. "Fats Waller and His Rhythm." *Jazz Hot,* no. 32 (July-August 1939):21. Record review of "If I Were You" and "Two Sleepy People."

Razaf, Andy. "Fats Waller." *Metronome* 60 (January 1944):16.

Schiedt, Duncan. "Fats in Retrospect." *Record Changer* 9 (December 1950):7, 16.

———. "Fats Waller." *Record Changer* 9 (September 1950):7, 12.

Schubart, Mark. "A Minority Report on Fats Waller's Concert." *PM Daily* 2, no. 15 (15 January 1942):24.

———. "Fats Waller to Give Jazz Recital in Carnegie Hall." *PM Weekly* 2, no. 30 (11 January 1942):57.

Schumach, Murray. "Interviewing Fats Waller and His Piano." *New York Times*, Sunday, 25 July 1943, section 2, 1, col. 4.

Sedric, Gene. "Trouping with Fats Waller." *Jazz Record*, March 1945, 10–11.

Stewart, Hector, and Asman, Jimmy. "A Tribute to 'Fats.'" *New Musical Express*, 16 May 1952, 13.

Taylor, J. R. "Fats Waller Strides Out of Sight." *Village Voice*, 1 August 1977, 47.

Traill, Sinclair. "Jivin' with Fats." *Melody Maker*, 11 September 1954, 13. Record review.

Waller, Fats. "Fats Says a Mouthful." *Jazz Journal* (through the courtesy of HMV), May 1952, 12. Reprinted in Shapiro and Hentoff, *Hear Me Talkin' to Ya*.

Wilkins, Roy. "Radio's Roly-Poly Organist." *Crisis* 41, no. 9 (September 1934):261.

Wilson, John S. "Five Months in the Musical Life of Fats Waller." *New York Times*, Sunday, 17 May 1981, section 2, 37. Record review.

———. "Waller Tribute by a Sextet Has Wit and Fervor." *New York Times*, 10 December 1977, 16.

3. Anonymous articles

"Banging the Piano for 8-Hour Stretches in Hollywood Has Made a 240-Pound Skeleton Out of Fats Waller." *New York World-Telegram*, 15 January 1938, 4.

"Fats Waller." *Current Biography 1942*. Edited by Maxine Block. New York: H. W. Wilson, 1942, 862–64.

"Fats Waller Demonstrates Swing, Even Defines It." *Metronome* 52, no. 2 (February 1936):19, 33.

"Fats Waller 'Learns' From European Bands." *New York World-Telegram*, 12 November 1938, 10.

Obituary. "T. W. (Fats) Waller. Pianist, Composer." *New York Times*, 16 December 1943, 27.

Obituary. "Fats Waller Rites Attended by 4,200." *New York Times*, 21 December 1943, 28.

Obituary. *Variety* 153, no. 2 (22 December 1943):54.

4. Liner notes for LP discs

Cooke, Roy, and Cangardel, Pierre-François; with Laverdure, Michel (for the "Memorial" and "Memorial no. 2" Boxed Sets), and Nevers, Daniel (for the "Fats Plus" volume). Notes to French RCA "Complete Recordings" of Fats

Waller (Black and White series): "Memorial" and "Memorial no. 2" Boxed Sets and 26 individual LP discs (see discography).

Francis, Harry. Notes to "Fats Waller in London." World Records Limited (EMI), SHB 29.

Lipskin, Mike. Notes to "Fats Waller Piano Solos, 1929–1941." Bluebird (RCA) AXM2-5518. Produced by Frank Driggs. N.B.: inaccurate matrix numbers are cited in the discography for this album for "Numb Fumblin'," "Smashing Thirds," and "My Fate Is in Your Hands."

McDonough, John. Notes to "The Fats Waller Story." Radiola 2MR–112113.

Montgomery, Michael. Notes to "Thomas (Fats) Waller: Parlor Piano Solos from Rare Piano Rolls." Biograph BLP 1002Q (vol. 1, 1923–1924), BLP 1005Q (vol. 2, 1924–1931), BLP 1015Q (vol. 3).

Morgenstern, Dan. Notes to "'Oh Mercy! Looka' Here.' Fats Waller, His Piano, His Rhythm—1935 & 1939." Honeysuckle Rose Records HR 5000-1, 5000-2, 5000-3. N.B.: the record number on the cover of this boxed set differs from the numbers printed on the labels of the discs themselves, cited above. The number on the cover is Honeysuckle Rose 5001.

Discography

This discography of Waller's recordings has two primary purposes: to list in chronological order all Waller recordings (including issued and unissued takes, accompaniments, radio broadcasts [many of which have only recently become available on LP], piano rolls, transcriptions, V-discs), and to provide where possible at least one LP source for those items that have been reissued. The chronology of the discography was determined by the date of recording, except in the case of piano rolls, for which date of release was used to establish each roll's place in the list.

Each item in the discography is identified by matrix and take number, title, and, where applicable, the manufacturer's number of the long-playing disc on which it may be found. (A key to these designations appears at the beginning of the discography.) Jazz LPs—especially those devoted to reissuing historical performances previously released on 78s—tend to be issued unpredictably, often by obscure labels or by companies incorporated outside the United States. These recordings do not ordinarily remain in print long. Thus, it is more than likely that by the time this discography is published, some of the albums listed will no longer be available outside libraries, archives, secondhand record stores, and private collections, and other albums, which might include items such as previously unknown recordings or pirated radio broadcasts—in other words, items that for some reason have remained hitherto unavailable—will have been released. For these reasons, I did not attempt a comprehensive listing of all LPs that include performances by Waller. Rather, I sought simply to distinguish those performances that had been issued (or reissued) on LP from those that had not, and thereby to establish at least one LP source where such performances might be located. There are, however, some exceptions to this general criterion: I do not include mention of LPs that have not been commercially available in recent years (issues of the RFW—Rarest Fats Waller—label, for example).

Some of the information in this discography, of course, appears in other sources: Brian Rust's *Jazz Records 1897–1942* (5th ed., 1982) is at present probably the most useful and important published reference for the jazz discographer, and much of the information compiled for my Waller discography was checked against Rust's authoritative and encyclopedic work. But Rust excludes from his Waller section those titles for which Waller was an accompanist or those for which Waller played in groups led by other musicians. Thus, as a comprehensive chronological listing, Rust's Waller discography is less useful, even though many of the recordings on which Waller plays a subsidiary role may be located elsewhere in the discography by using the index, which is cross-referenced. In addition, I have tried to fill the lacunae in Rust and to correct inaccuracies, although in both categories Rust leaves little to be desired. In all, Rust fails to include only sixteen alternate takes (for example, those for the 2 January 1941 session in Chicago), a few radio broadcasts that have been issued on LP since publication of *Jazz Records,* an occasional individual recording (e.g., the 28 September 1932 session at which Waller accompanied Monette Moore), and, of course, any recording that might have been made after July 1942. The inaccuracies, too, are minor: the matrix number for "Wherever There's a Will Baby," which Waller recorded with McKinney's Cotton Pickers on 7 November 1929, is 57140, as indicated for the second take in Rust's list (1034), not 57141, as indicated for the third take. (This error is probably typographical.) And in the titles listed for the 7 August 1939 session (1634), the item cited as "E Flat Blues" is actually a blues in B flat. (In fact, this error is not entirely Rust's responsibility; whoever originally supplied the title may simply have guessed at the key, and the resulting mistaken identification of the key as E flat has been perpetuated thereafter.) Other inaccuracies include the indication that Una Mae Carlisle participates as a vocalist on the second take of "I Can't Give You Anything But Love" recorded 3 November 1939 (matrix no. 043351-2).

For some sessions recorded by Victor I have been unable to resolve ambiguities in take numbers (and, in two instances, in matrix numbers—see 1 December 1927 and 18 December 1929 sessions). In such cases, a notation of the other possible take designation in parentheses, followed by a question mark, has been included. (These differences were unearthed by checking Rust's listing against those in *The Victor Master Book,* vol. 2 [1925–1936], also compiled by Rust. Obviously, there may be other discrepancies in take numbers after the year 1936.) Still other inconsistencies in take numbers surface in comparing the numbers cited in various album liner notes to those in *Jazz Records.* Almost invariably, Rust is correct. For example, the first Fats Waller Memorial boxed set of five discs issued by French RCA (RCA 730.570–730.574) includes a performance of "Smashing Thirds" (recorded 24 September 1929) that is identified in the liner notes for the set by the matrix and take number 56710-1. This version, however, is identical to that of the original 78 RPM recording, which is labeled 56710-2. Thus, "2" is the correct take designation, as cited in Rust.

Detailed indications of the instrumentation and personnel have been omitted; where Waller played only piano in sessions with a group not under his leadership or name, only the group's name is indicated, preceded by "With" (e.g., "With the Little Chocolate Dandies," 18 September 1929). If, either with his own group or with another, he sang on some takes, but only played piano on others in the same session, Waller's instrumental role for each take is stipulated in parentheses following the name of the group (e.g., "With Ted Lewis and His Band [piano]" or "With Ted Lewis and His Band [piano/vocal]," 5 March 1931). Likewise, if Waller performs on an instrument other than piano (usually pipe organ, electric organ, or celeste), this too is indicated in parentheses. If Waller's role (or that of his group) is primarily that of an accompanist, then the name of the singer or instrumentalist being accompanied has been included (e.g., "Piano, accompanying Monette Moore, vocal," 28 September 1932). Finally, Waller's pseudonyms or those of the principal performer on the recording are indicated in parentheses following the title.

I must recognize again the contributions to this discography made by Colby College student Glen Wright; his ability to feed this wealth of information into a computer and retrieve it in a thoroughly and logically organized format made the process of compiling this list an efficient and instructive one.

Those records designated "RCA" in the following list were all issued by French RCA; the abbreviation "B + W" indicates that the recording is included in French RCA's Black and White series.

RCA 730 570   "Fats" Waller Memorial (Boxed Set) vol. 1
RCA 730 571   "Fats" Waller Memorial (Boxed Set) vol. 2
RCA 730 572   "Fats" Waller Memorial (Boxed Set) vol. 3
RCA 730 573   "Fats" Waller Memorial (Boxed Set) vol. 4
RCA 730 574   "Fats" Waller Memorial (Boxed Set) vol. 5

RCA 731 054   "Fats" Waller Memorial no. 2 (Boxed Set) vol. 1
RCA 731 055   "Fats" Waller Memorial no. 2 (Boxed Set) vol. 2
RCA 731 056   "Fats" Waller Memorial no. 2 (Boxed Set) vol. 3
RCA 731 057   "Fats" Waller Memorial no. 2 (Boxed Set) vol. 4
RCA 731 058   "Fats" Waller Memorial no. 2 (Boxed Set) vol. 5

RCA 730 659   "Fats" Waller (Hitherto Unpublished Piano, Vocal and Conversation) (vol. 1) (B + W vol. 21)
RCA 730 660   Fats Waller Hitherto Unpublished Piano, Vocal and Conversation (vol. 2) (B + W vol. 22)

RCA 741 052   "Fats" Waller   Young Fats at the Organ vol. 1 (1926–1927) (B + W vol. 63)
RCA 741 062   "Fats" Waller with Morris's Hot Babies vol. 2 (1927) (B + W vol. 69)
RCA 741 076   Fats Waller   "Complete Recordings" vol. 3 (1927–1929) (B + W vol. 76)
RCA 741 086   Fats Waller   "Complete Recordings" vol. 4 (1929) (B + W vol. 85)
RCA 741 094   Fats Waller   "Complete Recordings" vol. 5 (1929) (B + W vol. 91)
RCA 741 112   "Fats" Waller   "Complete Recordings" vol. 6 (1930–1935) (B + W vol. 100)
RCA 741 113   "Fats" Waller and His Rhythm   "Complete Recordings" vol. 7 (1935) (B + W vol. 103)
RCA FPM1 7001   "Fats" Waller and His Rhythm   "Complete Recordings" vol. 8 (1935) (B + W vol. 113)
RCA FPM1 7008   "Fats" Waller and His Rhythm   "Complete Recordings" vol. 9 (1935–1936) (B + W vol. 111)
RCA FPM1 7025   "Fats" Waller and His Rhythm   "Complete Recordings" vol. 10 (1936) (B + W vol. 122)

RCA FPM1 7048 "Fats" Waller and His Rhythm "Complete Recordings" vol. 11 (1936–37) (B + W vol. 125)

RCA FXM1 7074 "Fats" Waller and His Rhythm Complete Recordings vol. 12 (1937) (B + W vol. 131)

RCA FXM1 7093 "Fats" Waller and His Rhythm Complete Recordings vol. 13 (1937/1938) (B + W vol. 136)

RCA FXM1 7123 "Fats" Waller and His Rhythm Complete Recordings vol. 14 (1938) (B + W vol. 140)

RCA FXM1 7166 "Fats" Waller and His Rhythm Complete Recordings vol. 15 (1938) (B + W vol. 148)

RCA FXM1 7198 "Fats" Waller and His Rhythm Complete Recordings vol. 16 (1939) (B + W vol. 157)

RCA FXM1 7282 "Fats" Waller and His Rhythm Complete Recordings (1939) vol. 17 (B + W vol. 164)

RCA FXM1 7316 "Fats" Waller and His Rhythm Complete Recordings (1939) vol. 18 (B + W vol. 169)

RCA PM 42027 "Fats" Waller and His Rhythm Complete Recordings (1939–1940) vol. 19 (B + W vol. 175)

RCA PM 42037 "Fats" Waller and His Rhythm Complete Recordings (1940) vol. 20 (B + W vol. 178)

RCA PM 42391 "Fats" Waller and His Rhythm Complete Recordings vol. 21 (1940–1941) (B + W vol. 183)

RCA PM 42396 "Fats" Waller and His Rhythm Complete Recordings vol. 22 (1941) (B + W vol. 186)

RCA PM 42416 "Fats" Waller and His Rhythm Complete Recordings vol. 23 (1941–1942) (B + W vol. 193)

RCA PM 43261 "Fats" Waller "Fats Plus" (1927–1943) (B + W vol. 202)

RCA PM 42407 RCA Jazz Tribune no. 7: The Complete McKinney's Cotton Pickers, vols. 1/2 (1928–1929)

RCA PM 43258 RCA Jazz Tribune no. 17: The Complete McKinney's Cotton Pickers, vols. 3/4 (1929–1930)

PMC 7038 Parlophone: The Chocolate Dandies

MRS #4 Meritt Record Society no. 4: The Piano Album

2MR-112113 Radiola: The Fats Waller Story (Personality Series No. 9–10; Release no. 112-113)

30 JA 5148 Jazz Anthology (Musidisc): Fats Waller 1939/1940 Private Acetates and Film Soundtracks

CC 10 Collector's Classics: Fats Waller on the Air

CC 19 Collector's Classics: Fats Waller 1935 & 1943

SHB 29 World Records Limited (EMI): Fats Waller in London

DE 601 Deluxe Records (Muse Records): "Fats" Waller Fine Arabian Stuff

HR 5000-1   Honeysuckle Rose Records (Boxed Set of 3 records): "Oh Mercy!
      Looka' Here" Fats Waller, His Piano, His Rhythm—1935 & 1939
HR 5000-2   Honeysuckle Rose Records (Second disc of above Boxed Set)
HR 5000-3   Honeysuckle Rose Records (Third disc of above Boxed Set)
BLP-1002Q   Biograph: Thomas "Fats" Waller 1923–1924 Parlor Piano Solos from
      Rare Piano Rolls
BLP-1015Q   Biograph: Thomas "Fats" Waller Rare Piano Roll Solos, vol. 3
CBS 66423   Columbia: Thesaurus of Classic Jazz. A Study in Frustration: The
      Fletcher Henderson Story
CBS 63366   French Columbia: Fats Waller   Fats Waller Plays, Sings, Alone and
      with Various Groups
SB 115   Sunbeam Records: Ted Lewis and His Band
XFL 15355   Commodore: The Liederkranz Sessions (Eddie Condon)
GJ 1029   Giants of Jazz: Fats Waller   Live at the Yacht Club

ca. 21 October 1922. New York.

Solo piano

  70948-D Muscle Shoals Blues (SHB 29)
  70949-D Birmingham Blues (SHB 29)

ca. 1 December 1922. New York.

Piano (as T. Waller), accompanying Sara Martin, vocal

  71068-C 'Tain't Nobody's Business If I Do
  71069-B You've Got Ev'rything a Sweet Daddy Needs but Me (Rust [1010, *Jazz
      Records*] lists this title as "You Got Ev'rything a Sweet Mama Needs But
      Me." But in the title on the Okeh label of the Martin recording the word
      "Daddy" is substituted for "Mama," and this is the way Martin sings it—not
      surprisingly, since she is presumably addressing the song to a man.)

ca. 14 December 1922. New York.

Piano (as Thomas Waller), accompanying Sara Martin, vocal

  71105-B Mama's Got the Blues
  71106-B Last Go Round Blues

ca. March 1923. New York. [For this and subsequent piano rolls, the date cited is date of release, not of recording.]

Piano roll

  QRS 2149 Got to Cool My Doggies Now (BLP-1002Q)

ca. May 1923. New York.

Piano roll

QRS 2213 Laughin' Cryin' Blues (BLP-1002Q)
QRS 2245 Your Time Now (BLP-1002Q)

May-June 1923. New York.

Piano, accompanying Alberta Hunter, vocal

1455-2 Stingaree Blues
1456-1 You Can't Do What My Last Man Did
1456-2 You Can't Do What My Last Man Did

ca. June 1923. New York.

Piano roll

QRS 2256 Snakes Hips (BLP-1002Q)
QRS 2270 'Tain't Nobody's Biz-ness If I Do (BLP-1002Q)

ca. July 1923. New York.

Piano roll

QRS 2286 Papa Better Watch Your Step (BLP-1002Q)

Piano, accompanying Anna Jones, vocal

1468-1 I Wish I Could Shimmy Like My Sister Kate
1468-2 I Wish I Could Shimmy Like My Sister Kate
1469-1 You Can't Do What My Last Man Did
1473-1 Trixie Blues
1473-2 Trixie Blues

ca. August 1923. New York.

Piano roll

QRS 2304 Haitian Blues (BLP-1002Q)
QRS 2322 Mama's Got the Blues (BLP-1002Q)
QRS 2331 Midnight Blues (BLP-1002Q)

ca. September 1923. New York.

Piano roll

QRS 2363 Last Go Round Blues (BLP-1002Q)

1 November 1923. New York.

Piano, accompanying Sara Martin and Clarence Williams, vocal duets

    71984-B I'm Cert'ny Gonna See 'bout That
    71985-B Squabbling Blues

ca. January 1924. New York.

Piano roll

    QRS 2444 You Can't Do What My Last Man Did (BLP-1002Q)

ca. May 1924. New York.

Piano, accompanying Porter Grainger, vocal

    31578 In Harlem's Araby

ca. 10 May 1924. New York.

With Jamaica Jazzers

    72514-A You Don't Know My Mind Blues
    72515-A West Indies Blues

5 August 1924. New York.

Piano, accompanying Hazel Meyers, vocal

    13467 Maybe Someday
    13469 When Your Troubles Are Just Like Mine

March 1926. New York.

Piano, accompanying Rosa Henderson (as "Mamie Harris"), vocal

    106735 You Get Mad
    106736 What's the Matter Now?

12 April 1926. New York.

(?) Piano, accompanying Alberta Jones Trio

    X-70 All God's Chillun Got Wings

13 April 1926. New York.

Piano, accompanying Caroline Johnson (as "Alta Browne"), with Bertha Powell, vocal duets

    X-71-A Nobody Knows de Trouble I See
    X-72-A Couldn't Hear Nobody Pray

22 April 1926. New York.

Piano, accompanying Elkins Negro Ensemble

   X-98 Wheel in a Wheel (Ezekiel Saw de Wheel)

23 April 1926. New York.

Piano, accompanying Caroline Johnson, vocal

   X-99-B Ain't Got Nobody to Grind My Coffee
   X-100 Mama's Losin' a Mighty Good Chance

3 November 1926. New York.

With Fletcher Henderson and His Orchestra (piano)

   142902-2 The Henderson Stomp (CBS 66423)

With Fletcher Henderson and His Orchestra (probably harmonium)

   142903-2 The Chant (CBS 66423)

17 November 1926. Camden, N.J.

Solo pipe organ

   36773-1 (or -3?) St. Louis Blues (RCA 730 570)
   36774-4 Lenox Avenue Blues (RCA 730 570)

With Six Hot Babies (pipe organ)

   36775-1 All God's Chillun Got Wings
   36775-2 All God's Chillun Got Wings
   36775-3 All God's Chillun Got Wings
   36775-4 All God's Chillun Got Wings

ca. January 1927. New York.

Piano, with Lewis Metcalf or Addington Major, cornet, accompanying Clarence Williams and Joe Sims, vocal duet

   2799-1 What Do You Know about That?
   2800-2 Shut Your Mouth

14 January 1927. Camden, N.J.

Solo pipe organ

   37357-1 Soothin' Syrup Stomp (RCA PM 43261)
   37357-2 Soothin' Syrup Stomp (RCA 741 052)
   37357-3 Soothin' Syrup Stomp (RCA 741 052)
   37358-1 Sloppy Water Blues (RCA PM 43261)

37358-3 Sloppy Water Blues (RCA 741 052)
37359-3 Loveless Love (RCA 741 052)
37360-1 Harlem Blues
37360-2 Harlem Blues
37360-3 Harlem Blues
37361-2 Messin' Around with the Blues (RCA PM 43261)
37361-3 Messin' Around with the Blues (RCA 741 052)
37362-1 Rusty Pail (RCA 741 052)
37362-3 Rusty Pail (RCA 741 052)
37363-1 I'd Like to Call You My Sweetheart

16 February 1927. Camden, N.J.

Solo pipe organ

37819-1 Stompin' the Bug (RCA 741 052)
37819-2 Stompin' the Bug (RCA 741 052)
37820-1 Hog Maw Stomp (RCA 741 052)
37820-2 (or -3?) Hog Maw Stomp (RCA 741 052)

Solo piano

37821-1 Black Bottom Is the Latest Fad
37821-2 Black Bottom Is the Latest Fad
37821-3 Black Bottom Is the Latest Fad
37822-2 Blue Black Bottom (RCA 730 570)

11 May 1927. New York.

With Fletcher Henderson and His Orchestra

144132-2 Whiteman Stomp (CBS 66423)
144133-3 I'm Coming Virginia (CBS 66423)

20 May 1927. Camden, N.J.

Solo pipe organ

38044-1 (or -2?) Sugar (RCA 741 052)

Pipe organ, accompanying Alberta Hunter, vocal

38045-2 (or -3?) Sugar (RCA 741 052)
38046-2 Beale Street Blues (RCA 741 052)

Solo pipe organ

38047-1 Beale Street Blues (RCA 741 052)

Pipe organ, accompanying Alberta Hunter, vocal

> 38048-2 I'm Goin' to See My Ma (RCA 741 052)

Solo pipe organ

> 38049-1 I'm Goin' to See My Ma

With Morris's Hot Babies (pipe organ)

> 38050-2 Fats Waller Stomp (RCA PM 43261)
> 38050-3 Fats Waller Stomp (RCA 741 062)

With Morris's Hot Babies (piano and pipe organ)

> 38051-1 Savannah Blues (RCA 741 062)
> 38051-2 Savannah Blues (RCA 741 062)

With Morris's Hot Babies (pipe organ)

> 38052-2 Won't You Take Me Home? (RCA 741 062)
> 38052-3 Won't You Take Me Home? (RCA 741 062)

early June 1927. New York.

Piano, accompanying Maude Mills, vocal

> 7295-1 I've Got the Joogie Blues
> Black Snake Blues
> Anything That Happens Just Pleases Me
> My Old Daddy's Got a Brand New Way to Love

14 November 1927. Camden, N.J.

Pipe organ, accompanying Juanita Stinette Chappelle, vocal

> 40077-2 Florence
> 40077-3 Florence (RCA 741 062)

Pipe organ, with Bert Howell, violin, accompanying Carroll C. Tate, vocal

> 40078-2 Gone But Not Forgotten—Florence Mills
> 40079-2 You Live on in Memory

Pipe organ, accompanying Bert Howell, vocal

> 40080-2 Bye-Bye Florence (RCA 741 062)

Solo pipe organ

> 40081-1 Memories of Florence Mills
> 40081-2 Memories of Florence Mills

1 December 1927. Camden, N.J.

With Morris's Hot Babies (piano and pipe organ)

  40093-1 He's Gone Away (RCA 741 062)
  40093-2 He's Gone Away (RCA 741 062)

Solo pipe organ

  40094-2 I Ain't Got Nobody (RCA 741 062)
  40095-1 The Digah's Stomp (RCA 741 062)
  40095-2 The Digah's Stomp (RCA 741 062)

With Morris's Hot Babies (piano, pipe organ and vocal—scat singing, one chorus only)

  40096-1 Red Hot Dan (RCA 741 062)
  40096-2 Red Hot Dan (RCA 741 062)

With Morris's Hot Babies (piano and pipe organ)

  40097-1 Geechee (RCA 741 062)
  40097-2 Geechee (RCA 741 062)
  40098-1 Please Take Me out of Jail (RCA 741 076)
  40098-2 Please Take Me out of Jail (RCA 741 076)

N.B.: *The Victor Master Book* indicates:

  40095-1 Red Hot Dan
  40095-2 Red Hot Dan
  40096-1 The Digah's Stomp
  40096-2 The Digah's Stomp

17 January 1928. New York.

Piano, with Howard Nelson, violin, and David Martin, cello, accompanying Andy Razaf (as Johnny Thompson), vocal

  145533-1 Back in Your Own Back Yard
  145534-3 Nobody Knows How Much I Love You

2 March 1928. Camden, N.J.

With Shilkret's Rhyth-Melodists (pipe organ)

  42529-2 (or -3?) Chloe (Song of the Swamp) (RCA 741 076)

3 March 1928. Camden, N.J.

With Shilkret's Rhyth-Melodists (pipe organ)

  42532-2 (or -3?) When You're with Somebody Else (RCA 741 076)

26 March 1928. New York.

With Dunn's Original Jazz Hounds

E-7232/3 What's the Use of Being Alone
E-7234/5 Original Bugle Blues

27 March 1928. Camden, N.J.

With Louisiana Sugar Babes (pipe organ)

42566-1 Willow Tree (RCA 741 076)
42566-2 (or -3?) Willow Tree (RCA 741 076)
42567-1 'Sippi (RCA 741 076)
42567-2 (or -3?) 'Sippi (RCA 741 076)
42568-1 Thou Swell (RCA 741 076)
42568-2 (or -3?) Thou Swell (RCA 741 076)
42569-1 (or -2?) Persian Rug (RCA 741 076)

18 June 1928. New York.

With Jimmy Johnson and His Orchestra

146539-3 Chicago Blues
146540-1 Mournful Tho'ts

1 March 1929. New York.

Solo piano

49759-1 (or -3?) Handful of Keys (RCA 730 570)

Fats Waller and His Buddies

49760-2 The Minor Drag (RCA 741 076)
49761-2 Harlem Fuss (RCA 741 076)

Solo piano

49762-2 Numb Fumblin' (RCA 730 570)

26 June 1929. New York.

Piano/celeste, with orchestra, accompanying Gene Austin, vocal

53586-3 I've Got a Feeling I'm Falling
53587-3 Maybe—Who Knows?

2 August 1929. Camden, N.J.

Solo piano

49492-3 Ain't Misbehavin' (RCA 741 076)

49493-2 Sweet Savannah Sue (RCA 741 076)
49494-1 I've Got a Feeling I'm Falling (RCA 741 076)
49494-2 I've Got a Feeling I'm Falling (RCA 741 086)
49494-3 I've Got a Feeling I'm Falling (RCA 741 086)
49495-1 Love Me or Leave Me (RCA 741 086)
49495-3 Love Me or Leave Me (RCA 741 086)
49496-1 Gladyse (RCA 731 054)
49496-2 Gladyse (RCA 741 086)
49497-1 Valentine Stomp (RCA 741 086)
49497-2 Valentine Stomp (RCA 730 570)

29 August 1929. Camden, N.J.

Solo piano

55375-1 Waiting at the End of the Road (RCA 741 086)
55375-2 Waiting at the End of the Road (RCA 741 086)
55376-1 Baby, Oh! Where Can You Be? (RCA 741 094)
55376-2 Baby, Oh! Where Can You Be? (RCA 741 094)

Solo pipe organ

56067-1 Waiting at the End of the Road (RCA 741 086)
56067-2 Waiting at the End of the Road (RCA 741 086)
56068-1 Baby, Oh! Where Can You Be? (RCA 741 086)
56068-2 Baby, Oh! Where Can You Be? (RCA 741 086)
56068-3 Baby, Oh! Where Can You Be? (RCA 741 086)
56069-1 Tanglefoot (RCA 741 086)
56069-2 Tanglefoot (RCA 741 086)
56070-2 That's All (RCA 741 086)

11 September 1929. New York.

Solo piano

56125-1 Goin' About (RCA 741 094)
56125-2 Goin' About (RCA 741 094)
56126-1 (or -2?) My Feelin's Are Hurt (RCA 730 570)

18 September 1929. New York.

With the Little Chocolate Dandies

402965-C That's How I Feel Today (PMC 7038)
402966-D Six Or Seven Times (PMC 7038)

24 September 1929. New York.

Solo piano

56710-2 (or -3?) Smashing Thirds (RCA 730 570)

30 September 1929. New York.

Fats Waller and His Buddies (accompanying the Four Wanderers, vocal)

56727-2 Lookin' Good But Feelin' Bad (RCA 741 094)
56728-1 (or -2?) I Need Someone Like You (RCA 741 094)

5 November 1929. New York.

With McKinney's Cotton Pickers (piano/celeste)

57064-2 Plain Dirt (RCA PM 42407)
57065-1 (or -2?) Gee, Ain't I Good to You? (RCA PM 42407)

6 November 1929. New York.

With McKinney's Cotton Pickers (piano/celeste)

57066-2 I'd Love It (RCA PM 42407)
57067-1 (or -2?) The Way I Feel Today (RCA PM 42407)
57068-2 Miss Hannah (RCA PM 42407)

7 November 1929. New York.

With McKinney's Cotton Pickers (piano/celeste)

57139-3 Peggy (RCA PM 43258)
57140-2 Wherever There's a Will, Baby (RCA PM 43258)
57140-3 Wherever There's a Will, Baby (RCA PM 43258)

18 November 1929. New York.

With Jimmie Johnson and His Orchestra (piano, possibly vocal, as one of "The Keep Shufflin' Trio")

57701-2 You Don't Understand (RCA 741 094)
57702-2 You've Got to Be Modernistic (RCA 741 094)

25 November 1929. New York.

Piano accompaniment (for Gene Austin)

57170-1 My Fate Is in Your Hands (RCA 741 094)

4 December 1929. New York.

Solo piano

> 57190-4 My Fate Is in Your Hands (RCA 741 094)
> 57191-1 (or -3?) Turn on the Heat (RCA 741 094)

18 December 1929. New York.

Fats Waller and His Buddies

> 57926-1 Lookin' for Another Sweetie (with Orlando Roberson, vocal) (RCA 741
>   094)
> 57927-3 (or -2?) Ridin' But Walkin' (RCA 741 094)
> 57928-1 (or -2?) Won't You Get off It, Please? (RCA 741 094)
> 57929-2 When I'm Alone (with Orlando Roberson, vocal) (RCA 741 094)

N.B.: *The Victor Master Book* indicates:

> 57926-3 When I'm Alone
> 57929-2 Lookin' for Another Sweetie

21 March 1930. New York.

Piano duet with Bennie Paine

> 59720-1 (or -3?) St. Louis Blues (RCA 741 112)
> 59721-1 (or -3?) After You've Gone (RCA 741 112)

30 October 1930. New York.

With McKenzie's Mound City Blue Blowers

> 10194-3 Girls Like You Were Meant for Boys Like Me
> 10195-1 Arkansas Blues

5 March 1931. New York.

With Ted Lewis and His Band (piano)

> 151395-2 Egyptian-Ella (SB 115)

With Ted Lewis and His Band (piano/vocal)

> 151396-1 I'm Crazy 'bout My Baby (SB 115)

6 March 1931. New York.

With Ted Lewis and His Band (piano/vocal)

151397-3 Dallas Blues (SB 115)
151398-2 Royal Garden Blues (SB 115)

13 March 1931. New York.

Solo piano/vocal

151417-3 I'm Crazy 'bout My Baby (And My Baby's Crazy 'bout Me) (CBS
63366)
151418-2 Draggin' My Heart Around (CBS 63366)

ca. June 1931. New York.

Piano roll

QRS 5143 I'm Crazy 'bout My Baby (BLP-1015Q)

14 October 1931. New York.

With Jack Teagarden and His Orchestra (piano/vocal)

151839-1 You Rascal, You (CBS 63366)
151840-1 That's What I Like About You (CBS 63366)
151840-2 That's What I Like About You

With Jack Teagarden and His Orchestra (piano)

151841-1 Chances Are
151841-2 Chances Are (CBS 63366)
151842-1 I Got the Ritz from the One I Love

10 November 1931. New York.

With Jack Teagarden and His Orchestra

10976-1 China Boy
10979-1 Tiger Rag

26 July 1932. New York.

With Billy Banks and the Rhythmakers (piano)

12119-1 I Would Do Anything for You (CBS 63366)
12119-2 I Would Do Anything for You

With Billy Banks and the Rhythmakers (piano/vocal)

    12120-1 Mean Old Bed Bug Blues (CBS 63366)
    12120-2 Mean Old Bed Bug Blues

With Billy Banks and the Rhythmakers (piano)

    12121-2 Yellow Dog Blues (CBS 63366)
    12121-3 Yellow Dog Blues
    12122-1 Yes, Suh! (CBS 63366)
    12122-2 Yes, Suh!

28 September 1932. New York.

Piano, accompanying Monette Moore, vocal

    TO 1210 A Shine on Your Shoes/Louisiana Hayride (MRS #4)

16 May 1934. New York.

Fats Waller and His Rhythm (piano/vocal)

    82526-1 A Porter's Love Song to a Chambermaid (RCA 741 112)
    82527-1 I Wish I Were Twins (RCA 741 112)
    82527-2 I Wish I Were Twins (RCA 741 112)
    82528-1 Armful o' Sweetness (RCA 741 112)
    82529-1 Do Me a Favor (RCA 730 571)

17 August 1934. New York.

Fats Waller and His Rhythm (piano/vocal)

    83699-1 Georgia May (RCA 741 112)
    84106-1 Then I'll Be Tired of You (RCA 741 112)
    84107-1 Don't Let It Bother You (RCA 730 571)
    84108-1 Have a Little Dream on Me (RCA 731 054)

28 September 1934. New York.

Fats Waller and His Rhythm (piano/vocal)

    84417-1 Serenade for a Wealthy Widow (RCA 730 571)
    84418-1 How Can You Face Me? (RCA 730 571)
    84419-1 Sweetie Pie (RCA 730 571)
    84420-1 Mandy (RCA 730 571)
    84421-1 Let's Pretend There's a Moon (RCA 730 571)
    84422-1 You're Not the Only Oyster in the Stew (RCA 730 571)

7 November 1934. New York.

Fats Waller and His Rhythm (piano/vocal)

    84921-1 Honeysuckle Rose (RCA 731 054)
    84922-1 Believe It, Beloved (RCA 741 112)
    84923-1 Dream Man (RCA 730 571)
    84924-1 I'm Growing Fonder of You (RCA 741 112)
    84925-1 If It Isn't Love (RCA 741 112)
    84926-1 Breakin' the Ice (RCA 741 112)

16 November 1934. New York.

Solo Piano

    86208-2 African Ripples (RCA 731 054)
    86209-1 Clothes Line Ballet (RCA 731 054)
    86210-1 Alligator Crawl (RCA 730 570)
    86211-1 Viper's Drag (RCA 730 570)

5 January 1935. Camden, N.J.

Fats Waller and His Rhythm (piano/vocal)

    87082-1 I'm a Hundred Per Cent. For You (RCA 741 112)

Fats Waller and His Rhythm (piano)

    87082-3 I'm a Hundred Per Cent. For You (RCA 741 112)

Fats Waller and His Rhythm (piano/vocal)

    87083-1 Baby Brown (RCA 730 571)

Fats Waller and His Rhythm (piano)

    87083-3 Baby Brown (RCA 741 112)

Fats Waller and His Rhythm (pipe organ/vocal)

    87084-1 Night Wind (RCA 741 112)

Fats Waller and His Rhythm (piano/vocal)

    87085-1 Because of Once Upon a Time (RCA 730 571)

Fats Waller and His Rhythm (pipe organ/vocal)

    87086-1 I Believe in Miracles (RCA 731 054)

Fats Waller and His Rhythm (piano/vocal)

    87087-1 You Fit into the Picture (RCA 741 113)

6 March 1935. New York.

Fats Waller and His Rhythm (piano/vocal)

88776-1 Louisiana Fairy Tale (RCA 741 113)
88776-2 Louisiana Fairy Tale (RCA 741 113)
88777-1 I Ain't Got Nobody (And Nobody Cares for Me) (RCA 731 054)

Fats Waller and His Rhythm (piano)

88778-1 I Ain't Got Nobody (And Nobody Cares for Me) (RCA 731 054)

Fats Waller and His Rhythm (piano/vocal)

88779-1 Whose Honey Are You? (RCA 731 054)

Fats Waller and His Rhythm (piano/celeste)

88780-1 Whose Honey Are You? (RCA 731 054)

Fats Waller and His Rhythm (piano/celeste/vocal)

88781-1 Rosetta (RCA 731 054)

Fats Waller and His Rhythm (piano/celeste)

88782-1 Rosetta (RCA 731 054)

Fats Waller and His Rhythm (piano/vocal)

88783-1 Pardon My Love (RCA 731 054)
88784-1 What's the Reason (I'm Not Pleasin' You) (RCA 741 113)

Fats Waller and His Rhythm (piano/celeste)

88785-1 What's the Reason (I'm Not Pleasin' You) (RCA 741 113)

Fats Waller and His Rhythm (piano/celeste/vocal)

88786-1 Cinders (RCA 741 113)
88787-1 (Oh Susannah) Dust off That Old Pianna (RCA 741 113)

11 March 1935. New York.

Solo piano/vocal, with Rudy Powell, clarinet

A-265 Baby Brown (RCA 730 659; HR 5000-1)

Solo piano

A-265 Viper's Drag (RCA 730 659; HR 5000-1)

Solo piano/vocal, with Rudy Powell, clarinet

A-265 How Can You Face Me? (RCA 730 659; HR 5000-1)

Solo piano

A-265 Down Home Blues (RCA 730 659; HR 5000-1)

Solo piano/vocal, with Rudy Powell, alto sax

A-266 Dinah (RCA 730 659; HR 5000-1)

Solo piano

A-266 Handful of Keys (RCA 730 659; HR 5000-1)

Solo piano with Rudy Powell, alto sax

A-266 Solitude (RCA 730 659; HR 5000-1)

Solo piano/vocal (except piano only, as noted)

A-267 I'm Crazy 'bout My Baby/Tea for Two (piano only)/Believe It, Beloved (RCA 730 659; HR 5000-1)

A-268 Sweet Sue/Somebody Stole My Gal/Honeysuckle Rose (piano only) (RCA 730 660; 5000-1)

A-269 Night Wind/African Ripples (piano only)/Because of Once Upon a Time (piano only) (RCA 741 113; HR 5000-1)

A-270 Where Were You on the Night of June the Third?/Clothes Line Ballet (piano only)/Don't Let It Bother You (RCA 730 660; HR 5000-1)

A-271 E-Flat Blues (piano only)/Alligator Crawl (piano only)/Zonky (piano only) (RCA 730 660; HR 5000-2)

A-272 Hallelujah (piano only)/Do Me a Favor/California Here I Come (piano only) (RCA 730 659; HR 5000-2)

A-273 I've Got a Feeling I'm Falling (piano only)/My Fate Is in Your Hands (piano only)/Ain't Misbehavin' (piano only) (RCA 730 659; HR 5000-2)

A-274 You're the Top/Blue Turning Grey Over You (piano only)/Russian Fantasy (piano only) (RCA 730 660; HR 5000-2)

N.B.: Rust (1626) indicates that the tune "How Can You Face Me?" was recorded at this session, coupled with the titles listed under the number A-274. But that title does not appear on either of the LP reissues of A-274.

8 May 1935. New York.

Fats Waller and His Rhythm (piano/vocal)

89760-1 Lulu's Back in Town (RCA 741 113)
89761-1 Sweet And Slow (RCA 741 113)
89762-1 You've Been Taking Lessons in Love (RCA 741 113)
89763-1 You're the Cutest One (RCA 741 113)
89764-1 I'm Gonna Sit Right Down and Write Myself a Letter (RCA 730 571)
89765-1 I Hate to Talk About Myself (RCA 741 113)

24 June 1935. Camden, N.J.

Fats Waller and His Rhythm (piano/vocal)

    88989-1 Dinah (RCA 730 571)
    88990-1 Take It Easy (RCA 731 054)
    88991-1 You're the Picture (I'm the Frame) (RCA 741 113)
    88992-1 My Very Good Friend the Milkman (RCA 730 571)
    88993-1 Blue Because of You (RCA 741 113)
    88994-1 There's Going to Be the Devil to Pay (RCA FPM1 7001)
    88995-1 12th Street Rag (RCA 730 572)
    88996-1 There'll Be Some Changes Made (RCA FPM1 7001)
    88997-1 Somebody Stole My Gal (RCA 730 572)
    88998-1 Sweet Sue (RCA 731 055)
    88998-2 Sweet Sue (RCA FPM1 7001)
    1935-1 Somebody Stole My Gal

2 August 1935. New York.

Fats Waller and His Rhythm (piano/vocal)

    92915-1 Truckin' (RCA FPM1 7001)
    92916-1 Sugar Blues (RCA FPM1 7001)
    92917-1 Just as Long as the World Goes 'Round and Around (RCA 730 572)
    92918-1 Georgia Rockin' Chair (RCA FPM1 7001)
    92919-1 Brother, Seek and Ye Shall Find (RCA FPM1 7001)
    92920-1 The Girl I Left Behind Me (RCA FPM1 7001)

20 August 1935. New York.

Fats Waller and His Rhythm (piano/vocal/celeste)

    92992-1 You're So Darn Charming (RCA FPM1 7001)
    92992-2 You're So Darn Charming (RCA FPM1 7001)

Fats Waller and His Rhythm (piano/vocal)

    92993-1 Woe! Is Me (RCA FPM1 7001)
    92994-1 Rhythm and Romance (RCA 731 055)
    92995-1 Loafin' Time (with Herman Autrey, vocal) (RCA FPM1 7001)

Fats Waller and His Rhythm (piano/vocal/celeste)

    92996-1 (Do You Intend to Put an End to) A Sweet Beginning Like This (RCA
        FPM1 7001)

Fats Waller and His Rhythm (piano/vocal)

    92997-1 Got a Bran' New Suit (RCA FPM1 7001)
    92998-1 I'm on a See-Saw (RCA 730 572)
    94100-1 Thief in the Night (RCA FPM1 7001)

ca. October 1935. Hollywood.

Fats Waller and His Rhythm (piano/vocal)

For film soundtrack *(Hooray for Love):* I'm Livin' in a Great Big Way (30 JA 5148)
For film soundtrack *(King of Burlesque):* I've Got My Fingers Crossed (30 JA 5148)

29 November 1935. New York.

Fats Waller and His Rhythm (piano/vocal)

98172-1 When Somebody Thinks You're Wonderful (RCA FPM1 7001)
98173-1 I've Got My Fingers Crossed (RCA FPM1 7008)
98174-1 Spreadin' Rhythm Around (RCA FPM1 7008)

Fats Waller and His Rhythm (celeste/vocal)

98175-1 A Little Bit Independent (RCA FPM1 7008)

Fats Waller and His Rhythm (piano/vocal)

98176-1 You Stayed Away Too Long (RCA FPM1 7008)
98177-1 Sweet Thing (RCA 731 055)

4 December 1935. New York.

Fats Waller and His Rhythm (piano/vocal)

98196-1 Fat and Greasy (RCA FPM1 7008)
98196-2 Fat and Greasy (RCA FPM1 7008)

Fats Waller and His Rhythm

98197-1 Functionizin' (RCA FPM1 7008)

Fats Waller and His Rhythm (piano/vocal)

98198-1 I Got Rhythm (RCA 730 572)

1 February 1936. New York.

Fats Waller and His Rhythm (piano/vocal)

98894-1 The Panic Is On (RCA 731 055)

Fats Waller and His Rhythm (celeste/vocal)

98895-1 Sugar Rose (RCA FPM1 7008)
98896-1 Oooh! Look-a There, Ain't She Pretty? (RCA 731 055)

Fats Waller and His Rhythm (piano/vocal)

  98897-1 Moon Rose (RCA 731 055)
  98898-1 West Wind (RCA FPM1 7008)
  98899-1 That Never-to-Be-Forgotten Night (RCA FPM1 7008)
  99035-1 Sing an Old-Fashioned Song (To a Young Sophisticated Lady) (RCA
      FPM1 7008)
  99036-1 Garbo Green (RCA FPM1 7008)

8 April 1936. New York.

Fats Waller and His Rhythm (piano/vocal)

  101189-1 All My Life (RCA FPM1 7008)
  101190-1 Christopher Columbus (RCA 731 055)
  101191-1 Cross Patch (RCA FPM1 7008)
  101192-1 It's No Fun (RCA FPM1 7008)

Fats Waller and His Rhythm (celeste/vocal)

  101193-1 Cabin in the Sky (RCA FPM1 7008)

Fats Waller and His Rhythm (piano/vocal)

  101194-1 Us on a Bus (RCA FPM1 7025)
  101195-1 Stay (with Elizabeth Handy, vocal) (RCA FPM1 7025)

24 May 1936. New York. (Radio Broadcast: The Magic Key Show)

Fats Waller and His Rhythm (piano/vocal)

  I'm Gonna Sit Right Down and Write Myself a Letter (CC 10; 2MR-112113)
  Christopher Columbus (CC 10; 2MR-112113)

4 June 1936. New York. (Radio Broadcast: The Rudy Vallee Show/The Fleischmann Hour)

Fats Waller and His Rhythm (piano/vocal)

  I've Got My Fingers Crossed (CC 10; 2MR-112113)
  Honeysuckle Rose (CC 10; 2MR-112113)
  Christopher Columbus (CC 10)

5 June 1936. New York.

Fats Waller and His Rhythm (piano/vocal)

  101667-1 It's a Sin to Tell a Lie (RCA 730 572)
  101668-1 The More I Know You (RCA FPM1 7025)

Fats Waller and His Rhythm (celeste/vocal)

101669-1 You're Not the Kind (RCA 730 572)

Fats Waller and His Rhythm (piano/vocal)

101670-1 Why Do I Lie to Myself About You? (RCA 730 572)
101671-1 Let's Sing Again (RCA 731 055)
101672-1 Big Chief De Sota (RCA FPM1 7025)

8 June 1936. New York.

Fats Waller and His Rhythm (piano/spoken commentary)

102016-1 Black Raspberry Jam (RCA FPM1 7025)
102016-2 Black Raspberry Jam (RCA FPM1 7025)
102017-1 Bach up to Me (RCA 731 055)
102018-1 Fractious Fingering (RCA 730 572)
102019-1 Paswonky (RCA 730 572)
102020-1 Lounging at the Waldorf (RCA 730 572)
102021-1 Latch On (RCA FPM1 7025)

1 August 1936. New York.

Fats Waller and His Rhythm (piano/vocal)

102400-1 I'm Crazy 'bout My Baby (RCA FPM1 7025)
102401-1 I Just Made up with That Old Girl of Mine (RCA FPM1 7025)
102402-1 Until the Real Thing Comes Along (RCA FPM1 7025)
102403-1 There Goes My Attraction (RCA FPM1 7025)
102404-1 The Curse of an Aching Heart (RCA FPM1 7025)
102404-2 The Curse of an Aching Heart (RCA FPM1 7025)
102405-1 Bye-Bye, Baby (RCA 730 572)

9 August 1936. New York. (Radio Broadcast: The Magic Key Show)

Fats Waller and His Rhythm (piano/vocal)

It's a Sin to Tell a Lie (CC 10)
Until the Real Thing Comes Along (CC 10; 2MR-112113)
I'm Crazy 'bout My Baby (CC 10; 2MR-112113)

9 September 1936. New York.

Fats Waller and His Rhythm (piano/vocal)

0339-1 S'posin' (RCA 730 572)
0340-1 Copper Colored Gal (RCA FPM1 7025)

0341-1 I'm at the Mercy of Love (RCA FPM1 7025)
0342-1 Floatin' Down to Cotton Town (RCA 731 055)
0343-1 La-De-De, La-De-Da (RCA 730 572)

29 November 1936. Chicago.

Fats Waller and His Rhythm (piano/vocal)

01801-1 Hallelujah! Things Look Rosy Now (RCA 731 055)

Fats Waller and His Rhythm (piano)

01802-1 Hallelujah! Things Look Rosy Now (RCA 731 055)

Fats Waller and His Rhythm (piano/vocal)

01803-1 'Tain't Good (Like a Nickel Made Of Wood) (RCA 731 055)

Fats Waller and His Rhythm (piano)

01804-1 'Tain't Good (Like a Nickel Made Of Wood) (RCA 731 055)

Fats Waller and His Rhythm (piano/vocal)

01805-1 Swingin' Them Jingle Bells (RCA 731 056)

Fats Waller and His Rhythm (piano)

01806-1 Swingin' Them Jingle Bells (RCA 731 056)

Fats Waller and His Rhythm (piano/vocal)

01807-1 A Thousand Dreams of You (RCA 731 056)

Fats Waller and His Rhythm (piano)

01808-1 A Thousand Dreams of You (RCA 731 056)

Fats Waller and His Rhythm (piano/vocal)

01809-1 A Rhyme for Love (RCA FPM1 7025)
01810-1 I Adore You (RCA FPM1 7048)

24 December 1936. New York.

Fats Waller and His Rhythm (piano/vocal)

03840-1 Havin' a Ball (RCA 730 573)
03841-1 I'm Sorry I Made You Cry (RCA FPM1 7048)
03842-1 Who's Afraid of Love? (RCA 730 573)
03843-1 Please Keep Me in Your Dreams (RCA 730 573)
03844-1 One in a Million (RCA FPM1 7048)
03845-1 Nero (RCA 730 573)

3 January 1937. New York. (Radio Broadcast: The Magic Key Show)

Fats Waller and His Rhythm (piano/vocal)

Hallelujah! Things Look Rosy Now (CC 10; 2MR-112113)
A Thousand Dreams of You (CC 10; 2MR-112113)

22 February 1937. New York.

Fats Waller and His Rhythm (celeste/vocal)

04949-2 You're Laughing at Me (RCA FPM1 7048)

Fats Waller and His Rhythm (piano/vocal)

04950-1 I Can't Break the Habit of You (RCA FPM1 7048)
04951-1 Did Anyone Ever Tell You? (RCA FPM1 7048)
04951-2 Did Anyone Ever Tell You? (RCA FPM1 7048)
04952-1 When Love Is Young (RCA FPM1 7048)
04953-1 The Meanest Thing You Ever Did Was Kiss Me (RCA 730 573)

18 March 1937. New York.

Fats Waller and His Rhythm (piano/vocal)

06413-1 Cryin' Mood (RCA FPM1 7048)
06414-1 Where Is the Sun? (RCA FPM1 7048)
06415-1 You've Been Reading My Mail (RCA FPM1 7048)
06416-1 To a Sweet Pretty Thing (RCA FPM1 7048)
06417-1 Old Plantation (RCA FPM1 7048)
06418-1 Spring Cleaning (RCA FPM1 7048)

31 March 1937. New York.

A Jam Session at Victor

06581-1 Honeysuckle Rose (RCA 731 056)
06582-1 Blues (RCA 731 056)

9 April 1937. New York.

Fats Waller and His Rhythm (piano/vocal)

07745-1 You Showed Me the Way (RCA 731 056)

Fats Waller and His Rhythm (piano)

07746-1 You Showed Me the Way (RCA 731 056)
07747-1 Boo-Hoo (RCA 730 573)
07748-1 The Love Bug Will Bite You (RCA FPM1 7048)

Fats Waller and His Rhythm (piano/vocal)

07749-1 San Anton' (RCA 731 056)

Fats Waller and His Rhythm (piano)

07750-1 San Anton' (RCA 731 056)

Fats Waller and His Rhythm (piano/vocal)

07751-1 I've Got a New Lease on Love (RCA 731 056)

Fats Waller and His Rhythm (piano)

07752-1 I've Got a New Lease on Love (RCA 731 056)

Fats Waller and His Rhythm (piano/vocal)

07753-1 Sweet Heartache (RCA 731 056)

Fats Waller and His Rhythm (piano)

07754-1 Sweet Heartache (RCA 731 056)
07755-1 Honeysuckle Rose (RCA FPM1 7048)

ca. April-May 1937. New York.

Solo piano/spoken commentary

The Gathering

Solo piano

Old Fashioned Love

Solo piano/vocal

I'm Crazy 'bout My Baby

Solo piano and piano accompaniment for other vocalists

Until the Real Thing Comes Along
I'm Comin', Virginia
Lost Love

Solo piano, with Gene Sedric, tenor sax

Blues Is Bad

9 June 1937. New York.

Fats Waller and His Rhythm (piano/vocal)

010647-1 (You Know It All) Smarty (RCA FXM1 7074)
010648-1 Don't You Know or Don't You Care? (RCA FXM1 7074)
010649-1 Lost Love (RCA FXM1 7074)

010650-1 I'm Gonna Put You in Your Place (And Your Place Is in My Arms) (RCA FXM1 7074)

Fats Waller and His Rhythm (piano)

010651-1 Blue, Turning Grey Over You (RCA 730 573)

11 June 1937. New York.

Solo piano

010652-1 Keepin' Out of Mischief Now (RCA FXM1 7074)
010653-1 Star Dust (RCA FXM1 7074)
010654-1 Basin Street Blues (RCA 731 057)
010655-1 Tea for Two (RCA 730 570)
010656-1 I Ain't Got Nobody (And Nobody Cares for Me) (RCA 730 570)

7 September 1937. New York.

Fats Waller and His Rhythm (piano/vocal)

013344-1 You've Got Me under Your Thumb (RCA FXM1 7074)
013345-1 Beat It Out (RCA 730 573)
013346-1 Our Love Was Meant to Be (RCA 730 573)
013347-1 I'd Rather Call You Baby (RCA FXM1 7074)
013348-1 I'm Always in the Mood for You (RCA FXM1 7074)
013349-1 She's Tall, She's Tan, She's Terrific (RCA FXM1 7074)
013350-1 You're My Dish (RCA FXM1 7074)
013351-1 More Power to You (RCA FXM1 7074)
013351-2 More Power to You (RCA PM 43261)

7 October 1937. New York.

Fats Waller and His Rhythm (piano/vocal)

014645-1 How Can I? (With You in My Heart) (RCA 731 057)
014646-1 The Joint Is Jumpin' (RCA 730 573)
014647-1 A Hopeless Love Affair (RCA FXM1 7074)
014648-1 What Will I Do in the Morning? (RCA FXM1 7074)
014649-1 How Ya, Baby? (RCA FXM1 7074)
014650-1 Jealous of Me (RCA FXM1 7074)

Fats Waller and His Rhythm, accompanying Dorothea Driver, vocal

014651-1 Call Me Darling

(?) 15 December 1937. Hollywood.

Piano, accompanying Peggy Dade, vocal

01446-1 Georgia on My Mind (RCA FXM1 7093)

16 December 1937. Hollywood.

Fats Waller and His Rhythm, accompanying Peggy Dade, vocal

   01445-1 On the Sunny Side of the Street (RCA FXM1 7093)

Fats Waller and His Rhythm (piano/vocal)

   09884-1 Every Day's a Holiday (RCA FXM1 7093)
   09884-2 Every Day's a Holiday (RCA 731 057)
   09885-1 Neglected (RCA FXM1 7093)
   09886-1 My Window Faces the South (RCA 731 057)
   09887-1 Am I in Another World? (RCA FXM1 7093)
   09888-1 Why Do Hawaiians Sing Aloha? (RCA FXM1 7093)
   09889-1 My First Impression of You (RCA FXM1 7093)

11 March 1938. New York.

Fats Waller and His Rhythm, and additional personnel (piano/vocal)

   02450-1 Marie (RCA FXM1 7093)

Fats Waller and His Rhythm (celeste/vocal)

   021150-1 Something Tells Me (RCA FXM1 7093)

Fats Waller and His Rhythm (piano/vocal)

   021151-1 I Love to Whistle (RCA FXM1 7093)
   021152-1 You Went to My Head (RCA FXM1 7093)
   021153-1 Florida Flo (RCA 730 573)
   021154-1 Lost and Found (RCA FXM1 7093)
   021155-1 Don't Try to Cry Your Way Back to Me (RCA FXM1 7093)

Fats Waller and His Rhythm (celeste/vocal)

   021156-1 If You're a Viper

12 April 1938. New York.

Fats Waller, His Rhythm and His Orchestra (piano)

   022429-1 In the Gloaming (RCA FXM1 7093)
   022429-2 In the Gloaming (RCA FXM1 7093)

Fats Waller, His Rhythm and His Orchestra (piano/vocal)

   022430-1 You Had an Evening to Spare (RCA FXM1 7093)
   022431-1 Let's Break the Good News (RCA FXM1 7123)
   022432-1 Skrontch (RCA FXM1 7123)
   022433-1 I Simply Adore You (RCA FXM1 7123)

022433-2 I Simply Adore You (RCA FXM1 7123)
022434-1 The Sheik of Araby (RCA FXM1 7123)
022434-2 The Sheik of Araby (RCA FXM1 7123)
022435-1 Hold My Hand (RCA FXM1 7123)
022435-1 Hold My Hand (RCA FXM1 7123)
022436-1 Inside (This Heart of Mine) (RCA FXM1 7123)
022436-2 Inside (This Heart of Mine) (RCA FXM1 7123)

1 July 1938. New York.

Fats Waller and His Rhythm (piano/vocal)

023760-1 There's Honey on the Moon Tonight (RCA FXM1 7123)
023761-1 If I Were You (RCA 730 573)
023762-1 The Wide Open Places (RCA FXM1 7123)
023763-1 On the Bumpy Road to Love (RCA FXM1 7123)
023764-1 Fair and Square (RCA FXM1 7123)
023765-1 We, the People (RCA FXM1 7123)

21 August 1938. London.

Fats Waller and His Continental Rhythm (pipe organ/vocal)

OEA-6383-1 Don't Try Your Jive on Me (SHB 29)
OEA-6384-1 Ain't Misbehavin' (SHB 29)
OEA-6384-2 Ain't Misbehavin' (SHB 29)

Fats Waller and His Continental Rhythm (piano/vocal)

OEA-6701-1 The Flat Foot Floogie (SHB 29)
OEA-6702-1 Pent Up in a Penthouse (SHB 29)

Fats Waller and His Continental Rhythm (piano/celeste/vocal)

OEA-6703-1 Music, Maestro, Please (SHB 29)

Fats Waller and His Continental Rhythm (piano/vocal)

OEA-6704-1 A-Tisket, A-Tasket (SHB 29)

28 August 1938. London.

Solo pipe organ/vocal

OEA-6385-1 Swing Low, Sweet Chariot
OEA-6385-2 Swing Low, Sweet Chariot

Solo pipe organ

OEA-6385-3 Swing Low, Sweet Chariot (SHB 29)

Solo pipe organ/vocal

OEA-6386-1 All God's Chillun Got Wings
OEA-6386-2 All God's Chillun Got Wings

Solo pipe organ

OEA-6386-3 All God's Chillun Got Wings (SHB 29)

Solo pipe organ/vocal

OEA-6387-1 Go Down, Moses
OEA-6387-2 Go Down, Moses

Solo pipe organ

OEA-6387-3 Go Down, Moses (SHB 29)

Solo pipe organ/vocal

OEA-6388-1 Deep River
OEA-6388-2 Deep River

Solo pipe organ

OEA-6388-3 Deep River (SHB 29)
OEA-6389-2 Water Boy (Convict Song) (SHB 29)
OEA-6390-1 Lonesome Road (SHB 29)

Pipe organ/spoken commentary, accompanying Adelaide Hall, vocal

OEA-6391-1 That Old Feeling (SHB 29)
OEA-6392-2 I Can't Give You Anything But Love (SHB 29)

13 October 1938. New York.

Fats Waller and His Rhythm (piano/vocal)

027289-1 Two Sleepy People (RCA 730 573)
027290-1 Shame! Shame! (RCA 731 057)

Fats Waller and His Rhythm (electric organ/vocal)

027291-1 I'll Never Forgive Myself (For Not Forgiving You) (RCA 731 057)
027291-2 I'll Never Forgive Myself (For Not Forgiving You) (RCA FXM1 7166)

Fats Waller and His Rhythm (piano/vocal)

027292-1 You Look Good to Me (RCA FXM1 7166)
027292-2 You Look Good to Me (RCA PM 43261)
027293-1 Tell Me with Your Kisses (RCA 731 057)
027293-2 Tell Me with Your Kisses (RCA FXM1 7166)

Fats Waller and His Rhythm (electric organ)

027294-1 Yacht Club Swing (RCA 731 057)

14 October 1938. New York. (Radio Broadcast: Yacht Club Program)

Fats Waller and His Rhythm (piano/vocal)

Yacht Club Swing (GJ 1029)
Hold My Hand (GJ 1029)
Pent Up in a Penthouse (GJ 1029)
Honeysuckle Rose (GJ 1029)
Yacht Club Swing (GJ 1029)
You Look Good to Me (GJ 1029)
St. Louis Blues (GJ 1029)
Flat Foot Floogie (GJ 1029)
After You've Gone (GJ 1029)
Yacht Club Swing (GJ 1029)

Solo piano

Hallelujah (GJ 1029)

18 October 1938. New York. (Radio Broadcast: Yacht Club Program)

Fats Waller and His Rhythm (piano/vocal)

You Could Be Mine (GJ 1029)
Monday Morning (GJ 1029)
What Do You Know About Love? (GJ 1029)
I Had to Do It (GJ 1029)

19 October 1938. New York. (Radio Broadcast: The Martin Block Program, Station WNEW)

Louis Armstrong, Fats Waller (piano), and ensemble

Honeysuckle Rose (RCA FXM1 7166)

Louis Armstrong, Fats Waller (piano/vocal), and ensemble

On the Sunny Side of the Street (RCA FXM1 7166)

Louis Armstrong, Fats Waller (piano), and ensemble

Tiger Rag (RCA FXM1 7166)
Jeepers Creepers (RCA FXM1 7166)

Louis Armstrong, Fats Waller (piano/vocal), and ensemble

> Blues (The Old Time Blues) (RCA FXM1 7166)
> I Got Rhythm (RCA FXM1 7166)

7 December 1938. New York.

Fats Waller and His Rhythm (piano/vocal)

> 030363-1 Love, I'd Give My Life for You (RCA FXM1 7166)
> 030364-1 I Wish I Had You (RCA FXM1 7166)
> 030365-1 I'll Dance at Your Wedding (RCA FXM1 7166)
> 030365-2 I'll Dance at Your Wedding (RCA PM 43261)
> 030366-1 Imagine My Surprise (RCA FXM1 7166)
> 030367-1 I Won't Believe It (Until I Hear It from You) (RCA FXM1 7166)
> 030368-1 The Spider and the Fly (RCA FXM1 7166)
> 030369-1 Patty Cake, Patty Cake (Baker Man) (RCA 731 057)

11 December 1938. New York. (Radio Broadcast: This Is New York, CBS Network)

Unidentified Orchestra (piano/vocal)

> The Joint Is Jumpin' (2MR-112113)

Unidentified Orchestra (vocal only)

> Summertime (2MR-112113)

Unidentified Orchestra (piano/vocal)

> Stompin' at the Savoy (2MR-112113)

19 January 1939. New York.

Fats Waller and His Rhythm (piano/vocal)

> 031530-1 A Good Man Is Hard to Find (RCA 731 057)
> 031530-2 A Good Man Is Hard to Find (RCA FXM1 7198)
> 031531-1 You Out-Smarted Yourself (RCA FXM1 7198)
> 031532-1 Last Night a Miracle Happened (RCA FXM1 7198)
> 031533-1 Good for Nothin' But Love (RCA FXM1 7198)
> 031533-2 Good for Nothin' But Love (RCA FXM1 7198)
> 031534-1 Hold Tight (Want Some Sea Food, Mama) (RCA 730 573)

Fats Waller and His Rhythm (electric organ/vocal)

> 031535-1 Kiss Me with Your Eyes (RCA FXM1 7198)
> 031535-2 Kiss Me with Your Eyes (RCA FXM1 7198)

6 February 1939. New York. (Radio Broadcast: The Broadway Showcase Program)

Piano/vocal, with unidentified small ensemble (probably Fats Waller and His Rhythm)

Old Grandad (2MR-112113; CC 10)

27 February 1939. New York.

Electric organ, accompanying Gene Austin, vocal

033993-1 Sweet Sue (RCA FXM1 7198)
033994-1 I Can't Give You Anything But Love (RCA FXM1 7198)

9 March 1939. New York.

Fats Waller and His Rhythm (piano/vocal)

032942-1 You Asked for It—You Got It (RCA FXM1 7198)
032943-1 Some Rainy Day (RCA FXM1 7198)
032944-1 'Tain't What You Do (It's the Way That Cha Do It) (RCA FXM1 7198)
032945-1 Got No Time (RCA FXM1 7198)
032946-1 Step Up And Shake My Hand (RCA FXM1 7198)
032947-1 Undecided (RCA FXM1 7198)
032948-1 Remember Who You're Promised To (RCA FXM1 7198)
032948-2 Remember Who You're Promised To (RCA FXM1 7282)

3 April 1939. London.

Solo piano/vocal, with Johnny Marks, drums

You Can't Have Your Cake and Eat It (RCA FXM1 7282)
Not There—Right There (RCA FXM1 7282)
Cottage in the Rain (RCA FXM1 7282)
What a Pretty Miss

12 June 1939. London.

Solo piano

Reminiscing through England, No. 2, Pt. 2

13 June 1939. London.

Solo piano (Most sources indicate Max Lewin, on drums, participated in this session. But only on "Bond Street" is the presence of drums a possibility.)

OEA-7878-1 London Suite-Piccadilly (SHB 29)
OEA-7879-1 London Suite-Chelsea (SHB 29)

OEA-7880-1 London Suite-Soho (SHB 29)
OEA-7881-1 London Suite-Bond Street (SHB 29)
OEA-7882-1 London Suite-Limehouse (SHB 29)
OEA-7883-1 London Suite-Whitechapel (SHB 29)
OEA-7884-1 Hallelujah
OEA-7884-2 Hallelujah
OEA-7885-1 Signing on at H.M.V.
OEA-7885-2 Signing on at H.M.V.

Solo pipe organ/vocal

OEA-7982-2 Smoke Dreams of You (SHB 29)
OEA-7983-1 You Can't Have Your Cake and Eat It (SHB 29)

28 June 1939. New York.

Fats Waller and His Rhythm (piano/vocal)

038207-1 Honey Hush (RCA FXM1 7282)
038207-2 Honey Hush (RCA FXM1 7282)
038208-1 I Used to Love You (But It's All Over Now) (RCA FXM1 7282)
038209-1 Wait and See (RCA FXM1 7282)
038210-1 You Meet the Nicest People in Your Dreams (RCA FXM1 7282)
038211-1 Anita (RCA FXM1 7282; RCA 730 574)
038212-1 What a Pretty Miss (RCA FXM1 7282)

(?) 16 July 1939. New York.

Fats Waller and His Rhythm (piano/vocal)

What's the Matter with You? (RCA FXM1 7282)

7 August 1939. New York.

Fats Waller and His Rhythm (piano/vocal)

ZZ-2143 The Moon Is Low (-1) (HR 5000-2)
         The Moon Is Low (-2) (HR 5000-2)
         Sheik of Araby (HR 5000-2)
         E-Flat (*sic:* B-Flat) Blues (incomplete) (HR 5000-2)
ZZ-2144 E-Flat (*sic:* B-Flat) Blues (HR 5000-2)
         Honeysuckle Rose (-1) (HR 5000-2)
         Honeysuckle Rose (-2) (HR 5000-2)
         Ain't Misbehavin' (HR 5000-3)

ZZ-2145 Sweet Sue (HR 5000-3)
    Nagasaki (HR 5000-3)
    I'm Crazy 'bout My Baby (false start) (HR 5000-3)
    I'm Crazy 'bout My Baby (HR 5000-3)
    Spider and the Fly (HR 5000-3)
ZZ-2146 Lonesome Me (HR 5000-3)
    After You've Gone (-1) (HR 5000-3)
    After You've Gone (-2) (HR 5000-3)

Solo electric organ

ZZ-2147 Dinah (partial) (HR 5000-3)

Solo piano

ZZ-2147 Poor Butterfly (HR 5000-3)
    St. Louis Blues (HR 5000-3)
    Hallelujah (HR 5000-3)
ZZ-2148 Tea for Two (HR 5000-3)
    [A] *(sic)* Handful of Keys (HR 5000-3)

The material from this date was remixed and coupled as follows:

ZZ-2143 Moon Is Low(-2)/The Sheik of Araby/E-Flat (*sic* B-Flat) Blues/
    Honeysuckle Rose(-2; spoken introduction deleted) (RCA 730 660)
ZZ-2144 Ain't Misbehavin'/Sweet Sue/Nagasaki/Lonesome Me (RCA FXM1
    7282; 30 JA 5148)
ZZ-2145 I'm Crazy 'bout My Baby/Spider and the Fly/After You've Gone(-2)/Tea
    for Two (RCA 730 660)
ZZ-2146 Poor Butterfly (RCA 730 659)
    St. Louis Blues (RCA 730 659)
    Hallelujah (RCA FXM1 7316; 30 JA 5148)
    A Handful of Keys (RCA FXM1 7316; 30 JA 5148)

10 August 1939. New York.

Fats Waller and His Rhythm (piano/vocal)

041528-1 Squeeze Me (RCA FXM1 7316; RCA 731 057)
041529-1 Bless You (RCA FXM1 7316)
041530-1 It's the Tune That Counts (RCA FXM1 7316)
041531-1 Abdullah (RCA FXM1 7316)
041532-1 Who'll Take My Place? (RCA FXM1 7316)

Fats Waller and His Rhythm (piano)

041533-1 Bond Street (RCA FXM1 7316)

3 November 1939. New York.

Fats Waller and His Rhythm (piano/vocal)

> 043346-1 It's You Who Taught It to Me (RCA FXM1 7316)
> 043347-1 Suitcase Susie (RCA FXM1 7316)
> 043348-1 Your Feet's Too Big (RCA FXM1 7316; RCA 730 574)
> 043349-1 You're Lettin' the Grass Grow Under Your Feet (RCA FXM1 7316;
>   RCA 731 057)
> 043350-1 The Darktown Strutters' Ball (RCA FXM1 7316; RCA 730 574)
> 043351-1 I Can't Give You Anything But Love (with Una Mae Carlisle, vocal)
>   (RCA FXM1 7316)
> 043351-2 I Can't Give You Anything But Love (Waller only, vocal) (RCA FXM1
>   7316)

15 November 1939. New York.

Piano, with Max Kaminsky's Orchestra, accompanying Lee Wiley, vocal

> P-26270-A I've Got a Crush on You

Pipe organ, accompanying Lee Wiley, vocal

> P-26271-A Someone to Watch Over Me

Piano, with Joe Bushkin's Orchestra, accompanying Lee Wiley, vocal

> P-26272-A How Long Has This Been Going On?

Piano, with Max Kaminsky's Orchestra, accompanying Lee Wiley, vocal

> P-26273-A But Not for Me

20 November 1939. New York.

Solo electric organ/vocal

> 043185-1 Go Down, Moses (DE 601)
>   Swing Low, Sweet Chariot (DE 601)
>   Hallelujah! I'm a Bum (DE 601)
>   Hand Me Down My Walkin' Cane (DE 601)
> 043186-1 Frankie and Johnny (DE 601)
>   She'll Be Comin' 'round the Mountain (DE 601)
>   Deep River (DE 601)
>   The Lord Delivered Daniel (DE 601)

Solo piano

> 043187-1 Ah! So Pure (*Martha*—von Flotow) (RCA FXM1 7316)
>   Then You'll Remember Me (*The Bohemian Girl*—Balfe) (RCA PM
>   42027; 30 JA 5148)

Sextet (*Lucia di Lammermoor*—Donizetti) (RCA PM 42027; 30 JA 5148)

My Heart at Thy Sweet Voice (*Samson and Delilah*—Saint-Saëns) (RCA PM 42027; 30 JA 5148)

043188-1 Intermezzo (*Cavalleria Rusticana*—Mascagni)

Solo piano/vocal

043188-1 When You and I Were Young, Maggie (DE 601)
Loch Lomond
Oh! Susannah (DE 601)
043189-1 The Old Oaken Bucket (DE 601)

Solo piano

043189-1 Waltz (*Faust*—Gounod)

Solo piano/vocal

043189-1 Annie Laurie (DE 601)
043189-1 Oh, Dem Golden Slippers (DE 601)

12 January 1940. Chicago.

Fats Waller and His Rhythm (electric organ)

044597-1 Swinga-Dilla Street (RCA PM 42027; RCA 731 057)

Fats Waller and His Rhythm (piano/vocal)

044598-1 At Twilight (RCA PM 42027)
044599-1 Oh! Frenchy (RCA PM 42027; RCA 730 574)
044600-1 Cheatin' on Me (RCA PM 42027)
044601-1 Black Maria (RCA PM 42027)
044602-1 Mighty Fine (RCA PM 42027)

Fats Waller and His Rhythm (piano)

044603-1 The Moon Is Low (RCA PM 42027; RCA 730 574)
044604-1 The Moon Is Low, Pt. 2 (RCA PM 43261)

11 April 1940. New York.

Fats Waller and His Rhythm (piano/vocal)

048775-1 Old Grand Dad (RCA PM 42027)
048776-1 Fat and Greasy (RCA PM 42027)
048777-1 Little Curly Hair in a High Chair (RCA PM 42027; RCA 731 057)
048778-1 (You're a) Square from Delaware (RCA PM 42027)
048779-1 You Run Your Mouth, I'll Run My Business (RCA PM 42027)

048779-2 You Run Your Mouth, I'll Run My Business (RCA PM 42027; RCA 731 058)
048780-1 Too Tired (RCA PM 42037)
048781-1 "Send Me" Jackson (RCA PM 42037)
048782-1 Eep, Ipe, Wanna Piece of Pie (RCA PM 42037)

16 July 1940. New York.

Fats Waller and His Rhythm (piano/vocal)

051865-1 Stop Pretending (RCA PM 42037)
051866-1 I'll Never Smile Again (RCA PM 42037)
051867-1 My Mommie Sent Me to the Store (RCA PM 42037; RCA 730 574)
051868-2 Dry Bones (RCA PM 42037)
051869-1 "Fats" Waller's Original E-Flat Blues (RCA PM 42037; RCA 730 574)
051870-1 Stayin' at Home (RCA PM 42037; RCA 730 574)
051871-1 Hey! Stop Kissin' My Sister (RCA PM 42037; RCA 730 574)

6 November 1940. New York.

Fats Waller and His Rhythm (piano/vocal)

057083-1 Everybody Loves My Baby (But My Baby Don't Love Nobody But Me) (RCA PM 42037; RCA 731 058)
057084-1 I'm Gonna Salt Away Some Sugar (For My Sugar and Me) (RCA PM 42037)
057085-1 'Tain't Nobody's Bizness If I Do (RCA PM 42037; RCA 731 058)
057086-1 Abercrombie Had a Zombie (RCA PM 42037)

Fats Waller and His Rhythm (celeste/vocal)

057087-1 Blue Eyes (RCA PM 42037)

Fats Waller and His Rhythm (piano)

057088-1 Scram! (RCA PM 42037)

Fats Waller and His Rhythm (piano/spoken commentary; accompaniment for Catherine Perry, vocal)

057089-1 My Melancholy Baby (RCA PM 42391)

7 November 1940. New York.

Fats Waller and His Rhythm (piano/vocal; from a film soundtrack)

Ain't Misbehavin' (with Catherine Perry, vocal) (30 JA 5148)
The Joint Is Jumpin' (with Catherine Perry, vocal) (30 JA 5148)
Your Feet's Too Big (30 JA 5148)
Honeysuckle Rose (30 JA 5148)

11 November 1940. New York.

With Eddie Condon and His Band, piano (as "Maurice")

    29054-1 Georgia Grind (XFL 15355)
    29054-2 Georgia Grind (XFL 15355)
    29055-1 Oh, Sister! Ain't That Hot? (XFL 15355)
    29055-2 Oh, Sister! Ain't That Hot? (XFL 15355)
    29056-1 Dancing Fool (XFL 15355)
    29056-2 Dancing Fool (XFL 15355)
    29057-1 (You're Some) Pretty Doll (XFL 15355)
    29057-2 (You're Some) Pretty Doll (XFL 15355)

31 December 1940. Chicago. (Radio Broadcast: Band remote from the Panther Room of the Hotel Sherman)

Fats Waller and His Rhythm (piano/vocal)

    Old Grandad
    Dark Eyes (CC 10; 2MR-112113)
    Jingle Bells (CC 10)
    Lila Lou (CC 10; 2MR-112113)

2 January 1941. Chicago.

Fats Waller and His Rhythm (electric organ)

    053794-1 Mamacita (RCA PM 42391)

Fats Waller and His Rhythm (piano/vocal)

    053795-1 Liver Lip Jones (RCA PM 42391; RCA 731 058)
    053796-1 Buckin' the Dice (RCA PM 42391)

Fats Waller and His Rhythm (piano/electric organ)

    053797-1 Pantin' in the Panther Room (RCA PM 42391; RCA 730 574)

Fats Waller and His Rhythm (piano/electric organ/vocal)

    053798-1 Come Down to Earth, My Angel (RCA PM 42391)
    053798-2 Come Down to Earth, My Angel (RCA PM 42391)

Fats Waller and His Rhythm (piano/vocal)

    053799-1 Shortnin' Bread (RCA PM 42391)
    053799-2 Shortnin' Bread (RCA PM 42391)

Fats Waller and His Rhythm (piano/electric organ/vocal)

    059100-1 I Repent (RCA PM 42391)

20 March 1941. New York.

Fats Waller and His Rhythm (piano/vocal)

    062761-1 Do You Have to Go? (RCA PM 42391)
    062762-1 Pan-Pan (RCA PM 42391)
    062763-1 I Wanna Hear Swing Songs (RCA PM 42391; RCA 730 574)
    062764-1 You're Gonna Be Sorry (RCA PM 42391; RCA 731 058)
    062765-1 All That Meat and No Potatoes (RCA PM 42391)

Electric organ/vocal (with guitar and drums)

    062766-1 Let's Get Away from It All (RCA PM 42391)

13 May 1941. New York.

Solo piano

    063887-1 Georgia on My Mind (RCA PM 42396; RCA 730 570)
    063888-1 Rockin' Chair (RCA PM 42396; RCA 731 058)
    063889-1 Carolina Shout (RCA PM 42396)
    063889-2 Carolina Shout (RCA PM 42396; RCA 730 570)
    063890-1 Honeysuckle Rose (à la Bach, Beethoven, Brahms, and Waller) (RCA
        PM 42396; RCA 730 570)
    063891-1 Ring Dem Bells (RCA PM 42396; RCA 730 570)

Fats Waller and His Rhythm (piano/vocal)

    063892-1 Twenty-Four Robbers (RCA PM 42396)
    063893-1 I Understand (RCA PM 42396)
    063894-1 Sad Sap Sucker Am I (RCA PM 42396)
    063895-1 Headlines in the News (RCA PM 42396)

1 July 1941. Hollywood.

Fats Waller, His Rhythm and His Orchestra (piano)

    061334-1 Chant of the Groove (RCA PM 42396; RCA 731 058)

Fats Waller, His Rhythm and His Orchestra (piano/vocal)

    061335-1 Come and Get It (RCA PM 42396)
    061336-1 Rump Steak Serenade (RCA PM 42396; RCA 731 058)

Fats Waller, His Rhythm and His Orchestra (piano)

    061337-1 Ain't Nothing to It (RCA PM 42396)

1 October 1941. New York.

Fats Waller and His Rhythm (piano/vocal)

067946-1 Oh Baby, Sweet Baby (What Are You Doing to Me?) (RCA PM 42396; RCA 730 574)

Fats Waller and His Rhythm (piano)

067947-1 Buck Jumpin' (RCA PM 42396; RCA 731 058)

Fats Waller and His Rhythm (piano/vocal)

067948-1 That Gets It, Mr. Joe (RCA PM 42416)

Fats Waller and His Rhythm (piano/vocal/bells)

067949-1 The Bells of San Raquel (RCA PM 42416)

Fats Waller and His Rhythm (piano/vocal)

067950-1 Bessie, Bessie, Bessie (RCA PM 42416)

Fats Waller and His Rhythm (electric organ)

067951-1 Clarinet Marmalade (RCA PM 42416)

21 December 1941. New York. (Radio Broadcast: Freedom's People Program)

Fats Waller, His Rhythm and His Orchestra (piano/vocal)

Honeysuckle Rose (CC 10; 2MR-112113)

26 December, 1941. New York.

Fats Waller and His Rhythm (piano/vocal)

068810-1 Winter Weather (RCA PM 42416)
068811-1 Cash for Your Trash (RCA PM 42416)
068812-1 Don't Give Me That Jive (RCA PM 42416)
068813-1 Your Socks Don't Match (RCA PM 42416)

10 January 1942. (Radio Broadcast on CBS; New York?)

Solo piano/vocal

Go Down, Moses (2MR-112113)
Ain't Misbehavin' (2MR-112113)

14 January 1942. New York. (Carnegie Hall Concert)

Piano/spoken commentary with Hot Lips Page, trumpet

Blues in B-Flat (2MR-112113)

Piano/spoken commentary, with Eddie Condon and His Band

Honeysuckle Rose

2 February 1942. New York. (Radio Broadcast [possibly Milwaukee]: Band remote from the Hotel Blatz)

Fats Waller and His Rhythm (piano/vocal)

Winter Weather (CC 10)
Cash for Your Trash (CC 10; 2MR-112113)

16 March 1942. New York.

Fats Waller, His Rhythm and His Orchestra (piano/vocal)

073440-1 We Need a Little Love (RCA PM 42416)
073441-1 You Must Be Losing Your Mind (RCA PM 42416; RCA 731 058)

Fats Waller, His Rhythm and His Orchestra (piano)

073442-1 Really Fine (RCA PM 42416; RCA 731 058)

Fats Waller, His Rhythm and His Orchestra (electric organ)

073443-1 The Jitterbug Waltz (RCA PM 42416; RCA 731 058)

13 July 1942. New York.

Fats Waller and His Rhythm (piano/vocal)

075423-1 By the Light of the Silvery Moon (with the Deep River Boys, vocal) (RCA PM 42416)
075424-1 Swing Out to Victory (RCA PM 42416)
075425-1 Up Jumped You with Love (RCA PM 42416)

Fats Waller and His Rhythm (quartet only), accompanying the Deep River Boys, vocal

075426-1 Romance à la Mode (RCA PM 42416)

30 July 1942. New York.

Vocal, accompanied by the Victor "First Nighter" Orchestra

075469-1 That's What the Well Dressed Man in Harlem Will Wear (RCA PM 43261)

ca. 1943. (exact date and location unknown)

Solo piano/vocal

Your Feets Too Big (2MR-112113)
[A] *(sic)* Handful of Keys (2MR-112113)

1943 (exact date and location unknown)

Solo piano/vocal

Ain't Misbehavin' (CC 10)
Handful of Keys (CC 10)

23 January 1943. Hollywood. (for the film *Stormy Weather)*

Piano/vocal, with the Twentieth Century–Fox Orchestra

That Ain't Right (CC 19)

Fats Waller and His Rhythm (piano/vocal)

Ain't Misbehavin' (RCA PM 43261; RCA 730 574)
Moppin' and Boppin' (RCA PM 43261; RCA 730 574)

16 September 1943. New York (V-Disc recording session)

Solo piano/vocal/spoken commentary

V-Disc 32-A (VP 154) Ain't Misbehavin'/Two Sleepy People (CC 19)
V-Disc 32-B (VP 155) (You're) Only Slightly Less Than Wonderful/There's a Gal
in My Life (RCA PM 43261; CC 19)
V-Disc 74-A (VP 157) This Is So Nice It Must Be Illegal/(There's Yes in the Air
In) Martinique (RCA PM 43261; CC 19)

Solo piano/spoken commentary

V-Disc 74-B (VP 181) Waller Jive/Hallelujah (CC 19)

Solo piano/vocal/spoken commentary

[Unissued] (VP 419) That's What the Bird Said to Me/You're A Viper (The
Reefer Song) (CC 19)

Solo piano/vocal

[Unissued] The Ladies Who Sing with the Band

Solo piano

[Unissued] To a Wild Rose/Don't Get Around Much Anymore

Solo electric organ/spoken commentary

> V-Disc 658-A (JDB 10) (In My) Solitude (RCA PM 43261; RCA 731 058; CC 19)
> V-Disc 630-A (JDB 11) Bouncin' on a V-Disc
> V-Disc 743-A (JDB 12) Sometimes I Feel Like a Motherless Child (RCA PM
>   43261; RCA 731 058; CC 19)
> [Unissued] St. Louis Blues
> [Unissued] By the Light of the Silvery Moon

23 September 1943. New York. (Radio Broadcast: "Personally, It's off the Record" program)

Solo piano/vocal

> Ain't Misbehavin' (2MR-112113)
> There's a Girl in My Life (2MR-112113)
> Honeysuckle Rose (2MR-112113)

Index

white musicians and, 4, 31
wit of, 4, 33, 70, 73, 81, 97
"Water Boy," 28 August 1938 session, 74
"(What Did I Do to Be So) Black and
Blue?," 4, 28
"When You're with Somebody Else," 3
March 1928 session, 46
Whiteman, Paul, 27
Williams, Spencer, 3, 87
"Willow Tree," 27 March 1928 session, 65–
68, 69
Wilson, Dooley, 6
Wilson, Teddy, 27, 30

WLW (Cincinnati), 78
"Won't You Get off It, Please?," 18
December 1929 session, 31–32

Young, Lester, 80
"You Rascal, You," 14 October 1931
session, 33
"You've Got Ev'rything a Sweet Daddy
Needs but Me," 1 December 1922
session, 12

Zanzibar Room, Hollywood, 6

DATE DUE
